Your First 100 Days

Lead Your Team in Your First 100 Days

Niamh O'Keeffe

PEARSON

Harlow, England • London • New York • Boston • San Francisco • Toronto • Sydney • Auckland • Singapore • Hong Kong
Tokyo • Seoul • Taipei • New Delhi • Cape Town • São Paulo • Mexico City • Madrid • Amsterdam • Munich • Paris • Milan

PEARSON EDUCATION LIMITED

Edinburgh Gate
Harlow CM20 2JE
United Kingdom
Tel: +44 (0)1279 623623
Fax: +44 (0)1279 431059
Web: www.pearson.com/uk

First published 2013 (print and electronic)

Pearson Education is not responsible for the content of third-party internet sites.

ISBN: 978-0-273-77678-9 (print)
       978-0-273-77917-9 (PDF)
       978-0-273-77918-6 (ePub)

British Library Cataloguing-in-Publication Data
A catalogue record for the print edition is available from the British Library

Library of Congress Cataloging-in-Publication Data
A catalog record for the print edition is available from the Library of Congress

ARP Impression 98
Printed in Great Britain by Clays Ltd, St Ives plc

Cover design by Dan Mogford
Print edition typeset in 11/15pt Myraid Pro Regular by 3

NOTE THAT ANY PAGE CROSS REFERENCES REFER TO THE PRINT EDITION

I would like to dedicate this book to all First100 clients.

Thank you.

Contents

Preface: First100™ www.First100assist.com ix
About the author xi
Acknowledgements xiii
Introduction xv

Part 1 Beginning 2

1 Prepare for your First 100 Days 5
1 Get organised: emotional focus and early research 6
2 Get your team ready for your arrival 14
3 Arrange a swift leadership handover 20
4 Understand the strategic context 22
5 What is your team mission? 24

2 Your First 100 Days Team Plan 29
1 First100assist™ Leader-Team Success Formula 30
2 Write your First 100 Days Team Plan 46

3 @start: Accelerate on arrival 55
1 Launch your First 100 Days Team Plan 56
2 Avoid the leader-as-hero trap 63
3 Bring in 'SWAT team' reinforcements 66
4 Speed up leader–team bonding 68
5 Advice from the executive front line 72

Part 2 Middle 76

4 @30 days: Optimise team performance 79
1 Review progress against team plan 80
2 Spot dysfunctional group behaviours 82

3   Capitalise on the strengths of the team 89
4   Update your First 100 Days Team Plan 93
5   Advice from the executive front line 94

5   @60 days: Sustain a strong momentum 97

1   Review progress against team plan 98
2   Remove barriers to high performance 101
3   Communication, communication, communication 108
4   Update your First 100 Days Team Plan 112
5   Advice from the executive front line 115

Part 3 End 118

6   @90 days: Sprint to the end 121

1   Review progress against team plan 122
2   Write your team's final 10-day 'to-do' list 124
3   Gather feedback and air any issues 127
4   Take time out for team reflection 136
5   Advice from the executive front line 142

7   Finish your First 100 Days 145

1   Close out your First 100 Days Team Plan 146
2   Record team achievements and capture lessons
      learned 148
3   Communicate team success to stakeholders 150
4   Celebrate with your team 151
5   Reset team objectives and renew the endeavour 153

Final words 157
Index 159

Preface: First100™
www.First100assist.com
EMPOWERING LEADERS TO SUCCEED IN THE FIRST 100 DAYS

First100™ are the specialist advisors to senior executives on how to achieve better and faster results in the first 100 days of a new leadership appointment.

First100™ background

Through my experience as a head-hunter placing senior executives in the City of London, I realised that the first 100 days were the most crucial stage in the lifecycle of a new leadership role appointment.

The first 100 days of a new role have a major determining factor on overall leadership performance and impact in the first 12 months and beyond. This is the time when you have optimal licence to refresh the vision, improve the strategy, re-form the team and set new goals. My observation was that failure to optimise the first 100 days was probably the biggest missed trick in leadership effectiveness and performance acceleration – a lost opportunity for the leader, resulting in losses for the inherited team and the organisation as a whole. My prior background of eight years as a strategy and management consultant for Accenture meant I was well equipped to convert this insight into a new niche 'first 100 days' leadership performance acceleration offering.

I set up First100™ in 2004 to create outcomes where everybody wins; a win for the newly appointed leader, a win for their team, organisation and market. I created a unique methodology and approach at First100™ that enables us to empower our client business leaders to step up and overcome the challenges inherent in the first 100 days of a new leadership role appointment.

First100™ clients

External hires – Internal promotions – Expat/Inpat rotations Maternity returners – Diverse hires & promotions

Our client track record of leadership performance acceleration in the first 100 days includes working with leaders from Telecommunications (BT, Eircom, Telefónica O2, Vodafone), Healthcare (Boston Scientific, BUPA International, Genzyme, Merck, Teva), Consultancies (Accenture, Oliver Wyman Group), Technology (AppSense, Microsoft, McAfee, Lionbridge), Financial Services (Barclays, Sun Life), Energy (BP), FMCG (Nestlé, Glanbia, John West) and many more. Client case study examples and a full list of First100™ services are available at www.first100assist.com.

About the author

Niamh O'Keeffe is the founder of First100™, established in 2004; www.first100assist. com.

> *'First100™ is a niche leadership performance acceleration consulting concept. We serve senior executives and CEOs in the first 100 days of a new leadership appointment.*
>
> *We provide our specialist 'First 100 days' consulting expertise using a unique combination of structured planning, leadership performance acceleration insights and strong results-orientation.'*
>
> *Niamh.Okeeffe@first100assist.com*

Niamh has a track record of over 20 years' career experience in leadership advisory services – including strategy consulting, executive search and leadership coaching.

Niamh is a transition-expert, problem-solver, idea-generator and trusted-advisor on leadership performance acceleration. Niamh's insights in this book are based on her many years of experience working as a leadership advisor and companion on the journey of senior leaders and CEOs in the first 100 days of a critical new leadership appointment.

Niamh is a business entrepreneur and very driven to succeed on her personal mission.

'My personal mission is to improve the quality of leadership in the world. We need our leaders to step up, perform better and act as more appropriate role models for the younger generation. I am delivering on my mission via the publication of leadership books and a portfolio of entrepreneurial businesses, the first of which was First100™ established in the UK in 2004.'

CEOassist is Niamh's second entrepreneurial business. It is a niche ideation and leadership advisory service for CEOs on how to develop optimal CEO Leadership Legacy Plans: www.CEOassist. com.

Acknowledgements

I would like to acknowledge my First100™ team, in particular Eimee, Fiona, Garrett, Padraig and Colm. I appreciate your dedication, hard work and support.

I would like to acknowledge Padraig Coffey's efforts on running the executive interviews process for the 'Advice from the executive frontline' sections of this book – and many thanks to the 40 plus senior executives who participated in the interviews and supplied us with great quotes and advice to share with readers.

A big thank you to the FT Publishing team at Pearson – always professional and a pleasure to work with. With special thanks to Nicole Eggleton, my editor, for her helpful advice and constant encouragement.

Finally, readers, I would like to acknowledge you. Please know that I appreciate how challenging it is to face into a new leadership role appointment. Thank you for reading this book.

Introduction

- Why is it important to build a high-performing team in the first 100 days?
- Why should you read this book?
- How to read this book
- The prequel: *Your First 100 Days: How to make maximum impact in your new leadership role*

Why is it important to build a high-performing team in the first 100 days?

Never before has there been so much pressure on newly appointed leaders to deliver better and faster results in the first 100 days. Not only is your first 100 days an early 'pulse check' on your leadership performance, taken by your boss and stakeholders, but it has become an early predictor and important determinant of your future career success. Do well in your first 100 days, and notice how quickly you will be offered expanded role responsibilities and faster promotion. Do badly in your first 100 days, and notice how quickly your portfolio of role responsibilities and allocated resources diminish and get reassigned to your peers.

This means that your ability to build and lead a high-performing team in your first 100 days has become a critical leadership skill. Your team represents the greatest opportunity for you to exponentially multiply and maximise all of your leadership efforts and insights. If you can get your team up and running quickly, and delivering fast results for you, then you are creating the optimal conditions for your longer-term leadership success.

get ahead and stay ahead
In this book, I explain how you can pro-actively take charge of leading your team and create a positive spiral of momentum towards leadership success right from the start. I advise you on how to get ahead and stay ahead.

There are numerous new pressures on leaders to build and lead a high-performing team in the first 100 days:

- Speed is the new competitive business weapon.
- Leadership role tenures have shortened considerably.
- Leadership role responsibilities have expanded considerably.
- Leading a team has become more complicated.
- 'Leadership change fatigue' has emerged as a new phenomenon.
- Your team's performance will make or break your reputation early on.

SPEED IS THE NEW COMPETITIVE BUSINESS WEAPON

To emerge intact from the global economic recession, organisations realise they need to deploy a faster-paced approach to making strategic decisions, fixing business operations and delivering results. Speed as a competitive business weapon has become a very important part of maintaining corporate stability, fueling growth and managing successful turnarounds. In today's economy, shareholders and boards expect their newly appointed leaders to perform ever better, ever faster. To deliver with speed, you need to have the ability to quickly galvanise and lead your team effectively in the first 100 days of every new role appointment.

Being new and requiring time to 'put your feet under the table' just doesn't cut it anymore. Cost-conscious investors want a fast return on their investment in you, and they don't expect to make concessions or wait around while newly appointed business leaders and their teams play catch up. From the moment you arrive, you need to be equipped and able to set a clear direction with your team, manage their time and resources effectively, and deliver fast results.

set a clear direction with your team and deliver fast results

LEADERSHIP ROLE TENURES HAVE SHORTENED CONSIDERABLY

Accelerating the performance of your team in the first 100 days is a new and necessary skill for fast-track leaders. Executive costs are high, role tenures have shortened and you need to learn how to demonstrate your value over a series of roles. Ambitious, fast-track leaders are expected to arrive, deliver maximum results in this role and then leave for the next step-up role more quickly than ever before. In global corporations, you are expected to be able to move on and re-create your efforts in another leadership role as soon as you have just fixed one business. Often leaders are given as little as two to three years within which to make their mark in one critical role appointment, before they are moved on to another role and another leadership challenge, and another first 100 days somewhere else in the same global corporation. Given this context, you need to add 'leading your team in your first 100 days' to your leadership skillset so that you know how to speed up the leader–team bond and high-performance dynamic, so that by the end of your role tenure you can show that you delivered on time, on budget and can more easily move on to your next role and next challenge.

LEADERSHIP ROLE RESPONSIBILITIES HAVE EXPANDED CONSIDERABLY

Role tenures have shortened and, at the same time, role responsibilities have expanded. Given the cost pressures over the last few years, many organisations have restructured and collapsed two roles into one new role. Perhaps this is the context for your new leadership promotion. For example, where there may have been a General Manager of Eastern Europe and a General Manager for Russia, now those two roles have merged into one role. How can one person do a role that previously required two people? Well, in today's climate you have no choice but to be on top of your game, right from the start. You need to be an even better leader, able to deliver more with less, and you need to be able to motivate your team to deliver ever more, ever better, ever faster.

in today's climate you have no choice but to be on top of your game, right from the start

LEADING A TEAM HAS BECOME MORE COMPLICATED

The complexity of highly matrixed organisations, and globally spread teams means that the relationship between the leader and the team has never been more challenging to establish. Ten years ago, the boss could walk the floor to get a sense of how the team was performing. Within 20 minutes, the leader could get a sense of the team's morale, its challenges and opportunities to improve performance. Nowadays, it is more likely that team members operate in different sites, different geographies and different time zones, and team meetings may be held only virtually. The pressure has increased, and the difficulty in comprehending team performance, let alone improving it, has increased exponentially.

You will have to consider direct reports, and your 'dotted line' reports, as well as other virtual team members and key stakeholders who you may rely on as members of your management team. As a newly appointed leader it becomes ever more difficult to create a sense of team when your key people are not in your office and not even in your time zone.

Add to this 'hot desking', 'home working' and part-time arrangements, and getting your team all in the same place even once a quarter becomes a near impossible feat – so even meeting your team members in person in the first 100 days may be a challenge in itself.

'LEADERSHIP CHANGE FATIGUE' HAS EMERGED AS A NEW PHENOMENON

There are numerous pressures on leaders: in addition to the pressure from the top down, you also face the bottom-up pressure from your inherited team who may be suffering from what I call 'leadership change fatigue'. Given the trend for shorter role tenures, many teams fail to ever establish themselves properly. Few teams ever come close to achieving their goals before the leader is switched and new goals are established under a new leadership reign. As such, teams are exhausted from these constant leadership switches. So it is more likely than not that whatever your new leadership appointment, the team is already jaded by the thought of the arrival of yet another new leader.

How to prepare and plan to tackle this emerging phenomenon takes extra care and attention in your first 100 days. After all, you are not going to achieve much if your team is already just exhausted at the thought of your arrival.

motivating your team will take a lot more effort than simply turning up and being their new boss

Motivating your team in your first 100 days will take a lot more effort than simply turning up and being their new boss.

YOUR TEAM'S PERFORMANCE WILL MAKE OR BREAK YOUR REPUTATION EARLY ON

Leaders cannot afford to forget just how much the team performance, attitude and results say to others about the person in charge. In your first 100 days, your key stakeholders will meet members of your team sooner and more often than they meet you. Their first impressions of you are being formed by their impressions of what it is like to work with your team members since you arrived. Also, at the start, everyone is curious about the new arrival, so your team will be asked by others for their opinions on you. If you have made a positive impression on your team, then they will be happy to let people know.

Remember that when your team members engage appropriately and perform well, it reflects well on you. When your team members over-promise and under-deliver, it reflects poorly on you. In the eyes of others, you are your team, and your team are you. It is a bit like how parents are judged on the manners of their children. You need to take charge of your team's 'manners' right from the start, so that you and your team present a united front and ensure that your stakeholders are satisfied that you have a joined up approach. Leverage your team to impress others and build their confidence in you. After all, your organisation, stakeholders and boss will invest more budget, more headcount, and more time in you, if they are satisfied that you and your team are credible, competent and can offer them a great return on their investment.

leverage your team to impress others and build their confidence in you

Why should you read this book?

Newly appointed leaders know that getting off to the right start with their team should be a critical priority in the first 100 days. However, the immediate time pressure and urgent day-to-day tasks often overwhelm the newly appointed leader's best intentions. As a result, my book is deliberately set up to keep your time and energy efficiently focused on how to build the right bond with your team and get off to an accelerated start in your new role.

I offer you a useful timeline structure on how to prepare in advance, and what to do at the critical milestones of @start, @30 days, @60days, @90 days.

- Chapter 1: Prepare for your First 100 Days
- Chapter 2: Write your First 100 Days Team Plan
- Chapter 3: @start: Accelerate on arrival
- Chapter 4: @30 days: Optimise team performance
- Chapter 5: @60 days: Sustain a strong momentum
- Chapter 6: @90 days: Sprint to the end
- Chapter 7: Finish your First 100 Days

Leading a team in today's pressurised environment may never have been so difficult, but it also has never been so exciting and so dynamic. With the right First 100 Days Team Plan in place, backed up with great insights and experience, I can help you to overcome adversities, take charge and be the master of your own success.

You should read this book if you are freshly appointed into a new senior leadership role and:

- face time pressures and an intense learning curve;
- want to make a high impact, and deliver ambitious results quickly;
- need your team to step up and impress key stakeholders;
- anticipate that there will be team legacy issues created by your predecessor;
- want to learn new approaches and new techniques on how to lead your team.

I will equip you with the appropriate leadership techniques and formulas in response to the challenge of how to lead your team in the first 100 days of a new role appointment. In this book, I will take you from the basic set-up arrangements with your new team through to the more sophisticated challenge of how you can truly develop a fast rapport and loyalty and organise the team for high performance to deliver on your role strategy.

By reading this book you have access to:

- First100™ insights and practical help;
- niche expertise of leading teams in the first 100 days;
- First100™ intellectual property;
- advice from the executive front line.

FIRST100™ INSIGHTS AND PRACTICAL HELP

This book is an aggregation of the insights and expertise we have accumulated at First100™. We are the global specialists on leadership performance acceleration in the first 100 days. Since 2004, we have worked with hundreds of leaders and teams. We have developed hundreds of First 100 Day Plans, across different industries and different geographies. We are global experts in the field of first 100 days, and we packaged up our insights to support you for leadership success with your team in the first 100 days.

NICHE EXPERTISE OF LEADING TEAMS IN THE FIRST 100 DAYS

Other 'leading-your-team' books are typically very generic, and not as expertly contextualised or targeted at the specific moment of need of how to lead your team in your first 100 days of a critical new leadership role appointment. I find that the books on building and leading teams are often aimed at new managers, i.e. first-time managers – rather than senior executive leaders. These books often make the assumption that your team is already in place, whereas in my book I appreciate that you are inheriting a team that may not yet be fully formed or fully equipped for a new leader and new team mission.

FIRST100™ INTELLECTUAL PROPERTY

In this book, I am pleased to share with you my First100assist™ Leader–Team Success Formula and my First100assist™ methodology on how to write a first 100 days team performance acceleration plan. I explain in detail what I mean by the seven-part formula for success on how a leader should build and lead a high-performing team in the first 100 days.

ADVICE FROM THE EXECUTIVE FRONT LINE

This book is peppered with fresh and recent First100™ client experience and insights from other executives who are not First100™ clients but who have their own experiences and advice to offer. We reached out and interviewed CEOs and other senior executives who are not clients of First100™ – in order to gather alternate perspectives on how they achieved success with their team in their first 100 days.

Readers of this book will learn how to:

- *consider the viewpoint of the team, as well as the viewpoint of the leader:*
  A leader needs to look beyond their own perspective and try to better understand the team's concerns, challenges and motivations. Rather than simply instruct the leader on what to do 'to' the team, I remind the leader of the importance of empathy and more sophisticated styles of team leadership – especially required for today's increasingly complex teaming structures and formations.

> **try to understand the team's concerns, challenges and motivations**

- *effectively manage the time invested in their team in the first 100 days:*
  This book offers a structured and disciplined process for setting out the right leader–team priorities in your first 100 days – and a structured and disciplined process for staying focused on these key priorities. My advice is divided into bite-sized chunks of insight, lined up with key timeline milestones that are served up to accommodate the reality of your time-constrained situation.

How to read this book

WHAT IS THE BEST WAY TO READ THIS BOOK?

Take this book on a train or plane ride, and aim to read from start to finish within 100 minutes. Once you have a total overview on the approach, go back and focus on the section that matters most to you at this moment in time. If you have not yet started in your first 100 days, focus on Chapter 1 on how to prepare and Chapter 2 on how to write your First 100 Days Team Plan.

HOW MUCH TIME SHOULD I SET ASIDE TO EXECUTE THE BOOK?

Having read the whole book as overview within your 100 minutes, my recommendation is that you then allocate approximately two hours of your time for planning and execution on each of the seven chapters. You don't need to invest all your time upfront. Invest your time wisely, as and when the milestone sections arise, so that the insights and information are more valid and applicable. Secure a great return on your time investment by building a high-performing team by the end of the first 100 days.

build a high-performing team by the end of the first 100 days

WHAT DO YOU MEAN BY 'FIRST 100 DAYS'?

For the avoidance of any doubt, let me explain that the First 100 Days refers to the actual number of calendar days following your official start date in your new leadership role. For example, if you start your job on 1 September, then your first 100 days will end on 9 December. However, feel free to give yourself a few days wiggle room because the first 100 days doesn't have to be totally literal. For example, in the case of a start date of 1 September, perhaps you could redefine your 100 days to end by the Christmas festive holidays.

WHAT DO YOU MEAN BY 'TEAM'?

For the purposes of this book, when I use the word 'team' going forward, I am referring to your key reports – a set of approximately three to ten key people upon whom you can rely on as your core group to get things done with their teams, and the rest of your people and organisation.

WHAT DO YOU MEAN BY 'EXECUTIVE ADVICE FROM THE FRONTLINE'?

What you read in this book is 99 per cent made up of my direct experience of working with First100™ clients. But I thought you would also find it interesting to hear directly from a range of senior executives across different companies, and different industries – all of whom were formally interviewed and welcomed the opportunity to look back and draw on their own experience of how to lead a team in the first 100 days. We interviewed over 40 senior executives for top tips and interesting insights on their experiences, and are pleased to present them to you at the end of every key milestone section of @start, @30 days, @60 days, @90 days.

The prequel: *Your First 100 Days: How to make maximum impact in your new leadership role*

As a newly appointed leader, you might find it useful to know that I wrote a prequel to this book, first published by FT Prentice Hall in 2011, called *Your First 100 Days: How to make maximum impact in your new leadership role.*

In that book I examined broadly the entire landscape of what leaders need to think about in their first 100 days, across person, role, organisation and market. I mapped out the 10 constituent roles inherent in any leadership role in the first 100 days (see Figure 0.1).

I used my experience-based First100assist™ methodology to describe how a leader can create his or her own compelling First 100 Days Plan by applying my First100assist™ 'whole system' framework to their new leadership role context, and by crafting

Figure 0.1 The 10 constituent roles inherent in any leadership role in the First 100 Days

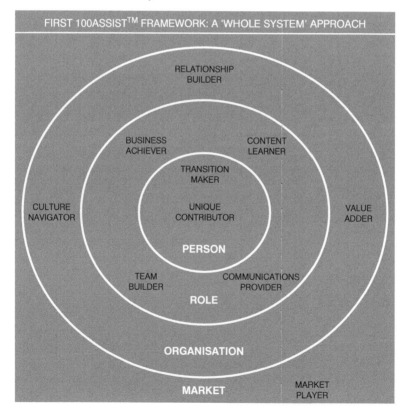

FIRST 100ASSIST™ FRAMEWORK: A 'WHOLE SYSTEM' APPROACH

RELATIONSHIP BUILDER

BUSINESS ACHIEVER

CONTENT LEARNER

TRANSITION MAKER

CULTURE NAVIGATOR

UNIQUE CONTRIBUTOR

VALUE ADDER

PERSON

TEAM BUILDER

COMMUNICATIONS PROVIDER

ROLE

ORGANISATION

MARKET

MARKET PLAYER

one key desired outcome to be achieved on each of the 10 constituent roles by the end of their first 100 days.

Your First 100 Days was a broad examination of the whole landscape of the 10 key constituent roles and leadership priorities in the first 100 days. Following its publication and unprecedented positive response by readers, it was clear to me that readers had an appetite for a more in-depth examination of each of the 10 constituent roles, and so I have set out this book to be a more in-depth investigation of a 'team builder' and how to build and accelerate a high-performing team in the first 100 days. Building your team is arguably the number one priority for any newly appointed leader. After all, you cannot be a successful leader if you don't have a strong and capable team followership.

Each book can be read as a value-adding, standalone, useful and insightful read. I recommend that you read both, so that you have the benefit of a broad leadership perspective and an in-depth team perspective on the first 100 days. The material is different in each book, and the topics merge seamlessly so that the books are complementary. *Your First 100 Days* provides the broad overview on everything to be done by a newly appointed leader in the first 100 days, and *Lead Your Team in Your First 100 Days* provides an in-depth examination on the one specific priority of how to lead your team and accelerate team performance in the first 100 days.

part one

Beginning

Prepare for your First 100 Days

- Get organised: emotional focus and early research
- Get your team ready for your arrival
- Arrange a swift leadership handover
- Understand the strategic context
- What is your team mission?

1 Get organised: emotional focus and early research

Building and leading a high-performing team will be critical to your success in the first 100 days. As soon as your new role appointment has been agreed, and even as the ink is still drying on your contract, there will be a list of a thousand things to do running through your mind. In terms of key strategic priorities, one of the most important tasks ahead of you is how to take charge and lead your team in the first 100 days.

Establishing yourself as leader of a team can feel like a daunting task:

- Do I have the right people?
- What challenges lie ahead?
- Will I make a good impression?
- How will the team respond to me?
- What do they expect from me as their new boss?

what do they expect from me as their new boss?

Whenever we are faced with an overwhelming situation, the best thing to do is take a step back, take a deep breath and get organised. I advise my clients to get perspective and take control by engaging and paying attention to both the right and left side of the brain. What I mean by this is to use your right brain to acknowledge and manage your emotional state, and in parallel employ your left brain to gather the data and information that you need.

- Right brain: emotional focus
- Left brain: early research

EMOTIONAL FOCUS

Acknowledge your feelings and manage your emotions

Getting ready to lead a new team is a heightened stress situation. Unfortunately many senior executives respond to stress by trying to deny its very existence. Rather than numb yourself to the uncomfortable aspects of the reality of your situation, and rather than block out feelings, try to deal with them instead. Master the ability to turn that nervous anxiety into a more constructive positive mental state. To stay in control, you need to acknowledge and deal with your feelings as they arise. This comes under the larger discussion on the topic of the importance of emotional intelligence for leaders, in particular in self-awareness and self-regulation. Reassure yourself that of course it is natural that getting ready to lead your team will stir up emotions that span the spectrum of confident excitement to nervous anxiety.

The hierarchy requirement whereby you need to establish yourself as the boss and command respect from others – some former peers – can make some people feel very apprehensive. If that is the case for you, perhaps you would find it useful to open up a discussion on how you are feeling with a trusted advisor or friend. Most people feel this tension, so you need to be ready to find a way to regulate your emotions, and seek a calm and neutral emotional state. This enables you to be clear-headed and focused on the task of optimal first 100 days planning, developing your entry tactics and conducting early research on the team.

Empathise with your team's emotions

Realise that your team members are also having emotional feelings about your arrival as their new boss. It can really help your own perspective, if you think about things from the perspective of the other party. Understanding how your team might be feeling at this stage is also the important beginning of your empathetic relationship with them, and will help accelerate leader–team bonding.

Let's take a sneak peek into the mind of your team, to see what they are thinking right now:

- Who is this person?
- Will I like him/her?
- Will s/he like me?
- Why did s/he get the job?
- Why didn't I get the job?
- What does this mean for my career?
- Will I bother to stick around (the defence strategy: *'if I don't like him, I am going to leave!'*)?

leave room for building empathy and considering the feelings of others

You're not the only one with emotional reactions and concerns about this relationship. Remember you have got the job, but these guys don't know if they will still have their job in three months' time. Bear that in mind, so that you don't become overly consumed by your own emotions. Leave room for building empathy and considering the feelings of others too.

Recommit to being the best leader you can be

Get in touch with your emotional feelings to re-ignite your hopes, dreams, aspirations for the future and your leadership legacy. Every new beginning is an opportunity to reset and renew yourself as a leader.

Decide what kind of leader you want to be with this team. Take the time to reflect on how you have led teams in the past.

- What were your greatest strengths when you led a team?
- What feedback did you get from the team and others on your areas for improvement?
- What leaders do you admire and might you try to emulate in this new role?
- What do you want to change about your leadership style and skills for this new team?

This is a fresh opportunity to improve and to be the best leader you can be. You could re-engage with your own values and your own personal brand, and recommit.

this is a fresh opportunity to improve and to be the best leader you can be

For example, I commit to having:

- more courage to take risks, make faster and better decisions, and lead the team forward;
- more compassion on giving people a second chance and equipping them for success;
- more time and energy invested to direct, coach, guide and support the team.

Take time out to relax and rejuvenate

I would like you to invest time now in preparing adequately for a strong start in leading your team in the first 100 days. But part of that preparation involves taking some time out to relax and rejuvenate before you start this new role, especially if you have a lot of nervous energy. You need to have a lot of mental and physical energy for leading your team in the first 100 days. This may be a team that has been without a leader for several months whilst waiting for your arrival.

Even if there is a leader in place, it may have been an interim arrangement or may not have been working – as otherwise you would not be in post. So the team will likely be 'needy' and may even be expecting you to 'save them' and lead them out of a crisis. You need to ensure that your energy reserves are topped up and that your expectations are set that the team is going to take up a lot of your energy in the first 100 days. It always surprises me how much my clients underestimate this. It's as if they think that their team will simply get on with business as usual. Whereas in reality the needs of the team can be overwhelming and time consuming – and you need to ensure that you are in good enough shape emotionally and energetically to deal with their needs whilst catering for your own needs too.

EARLY RESEARCH

Scope out the size, shape and quality of your team

One of your first tasks as a newly appointed leader may be how to figure out exactly who you have inherited, how many and whether they meet your standard for what you want from your core team. Working with your boss and your HR person, you can do a lot of advance research on what you are inheriting. It gives you a sense of what you've got, before you meet any of them. This information will also give you a sense of what you've got versus what you may need.

who is on my team?

Who is on my team?

- Names and biographies of key reports.
- Team organisation structure chart, with titles and names.
- How many direct reports, dotted lines and virtual team members?

- How many in your total charge, in terms of key reports and below?
- Geographic spread, full-time versus part-time, any home-workers, any maternity leavers.
- Previously gathered psychometric or behavioural profiles of individuals, or of the team.
- Last round of performance appraisals and rankings of each person.
- Are there known gaps and role vacancies on the team?
- What recruitment activities or executive searches, if any, are underway?
- How much scope do you have to bring in fresh talent to the team – from internal pool, and from external market?

Don't assume that just because they are your inherited team, that you can't change the structure and composition of your key report team. It is most likely that as you get a sense of the challenges ahead and clarity on your team mission that you will want to make changes and re-establish your core team, but for now, just get a sense of the current picture and current situation.

Get a handle on corporate HR processes and the annual cycle of performance appraisals

As you know, companies have an annual system of performance appraisals, preset to specific months and dates in the calendar year – and the system rolls on, regardless of what suits your preferred timings. You are best served if you know in advance when it is going to happen, and what is required of you. You might be lucky and arrive just as it is completing so that your predecessor handled it, but I have known instances where my client arrived right in the middle of the process and folks were simply expecting him/her to pick up and run with it. You will have so much to do in your first 100 days and first six months, on so many fronts, that dealing with the corporate performance appraisal process and systems is not something that you want to be blind-sided by. It is best to ask questions now and try to figure it all out, in advance.

- When is the company's annual performance appraisal cycle?
- When will responsibility for team member performance appraisals be fully handed over to you?
- Who, on your team, is in line for promotion, and what is the HR view on the performance and potential of each individual?
- What frameworks/key competencies/values-based criteria and ranking types are used to conduct performance appraisals – at each pay grade?

Debrief with your hiring manager (i.e. your boss)

In addition to the scoping information you can gather on the team, it is always useful to get a heads up from your hiring manager because they hired you with a situational context in mind. The decision to hire you was set in a context which you now need to seek to more fully understand.

- What are the perceived strengths and weaknesses of individuals and how do they work as a team?
- What are the legacy issues that you should know about?
- Who is currently leading the team, and why, and for how long?
- Will your predecessor still be there when you arrive? (More on this later.)
- Who went for your job? (Is that person now feeling demotivated and resentful of your arrival?)

● Any other heads up, regarding history of the team or team members that you should know about?

It is always useful to get the inside track on what your boss thinks, but you don't need to take everything that is said at face value. It is too early to form any fixed views on anyone you have not yet met, or interacted with. Don't be too easily influenced by your boss. Stay in your own space and don't form quick judgements until you have the experience of meeting and working with someone yourself.

stay in your own space and don't form quick judgements

Find out how your competitor teams shape up

In some situations, organisations will have built up some informal knowledge of competitor team behaviour – particularly in consulting or sales bid environments where it is easier to find out what the competition is up to. For example, when consulting firms lose a bid, then in the post-bid mop-up it is entirely acceptable to ask what was better about the other side. Either in advance, or during your first 100 days, you could try to tap into this knowledge of the competition. If the competition is outbidding your team again and again, then they must be doing something

Table 1.1 Get organised: emotional focus, early research

Emotional focus	– Acknowledge your feelings and manage your emotions. – Empathise with your team's emotions. – Recommit to being the best leader you can be. – Take time out to relax and rejuvenate.
Early research	– Scope out the size, shape and quality of your team. – Get a handle on corporate HR processes and the annual cycle of performance appraisals. – Debrief with your hiring manager. – Find out how your competitor teams shape up.

right – so let's learn from it. Perhaps they are incentivised in a different way, and this might give you the idea of changing the incentive model with your team as part of change you wish to make by the end of your first 100 days.

2 Get your team ready for your arrival

In the same way that you have a set of tasks that help you prepare to lead the team, there is no reason why you cannot arrange for a set of tasks to be given to the team to help them prepare for their new leader. If you and your team are adequately prepared in advance of your arrival, then you are all off to a fast and focused start.

- Ask the team to prepare a presentation.
- Write a pre-arrival memo.
- Meet the team informally.

ASK THE TEAM TO PREPARE A PRESENTATION

Ask your hiring manager – or your PA, if you have one – to schedule a 45-minute one-to-one meeting with each of your direct reports to be held in the first two weeks of your arrival. Request that each of your direct report team members prepare a presentation for you, covering the following information on their key area of responsibility:

My role and key areas of responsibility

- Role description
- Role targets and key objectives
- Recent successes, key challenges and opportunities
- Options and ideas for immediate quick wins
- Role stakeholders, and how my role is perceived in the organisation
- My individual performance objectives
- My career aspiration and ambitions
- If I were CEO for a day, I would...
- Ideas for shaping the leader's team agenda

(maximum 10 pages)

Naturally, feel free to adjust the list to suit the language and context of your own situation. This exercise will be a good way to take an early read on the quality of your team. It is quite an open-ended brief and some members will really step up to this task, whilst others may not. **who is showing good will?**

When you meet them to hear their presentation, you will be able to answer the following questions:

- Who is showing goodwill in terms of how they approached the task, and level of passion/commitment?
- Who has baggage, and who has left it at the door? In other words, some team members may focus on the challenges whereas others may see more of the opportunities. The former is not necessarily a problem, but ideally you want a healthy balanced perspective.
- Who has good ideas? The sooner you hear good ideas

the better for you too. The good ideas from existing team members could be the 'low hanging fruit' of easily implementable quick wins that may help you have early impact/results.

● Who is presenting an honest and realistic game plan?

who is presenting an honest and realistic game plan?

From role discussions with the hiring manager you will already have a sense of the challenges, opportunities and next steps, and can sense-check what you are now hearing from your team members.

In addition to ensuring your team is getting ready for your arrival, by asking for this exercise to be completed, you are also signalling that you are making a fast start, that you are in listening mode and that you respect the views of the team members. It also signals that you have high expectations of the team, and that you expect them to have a contributing voice, and that this leadership transition is not going to be business as usual. Your high performers will welcome this, and anyone who is not up for the challenge may (hopefully!) decide to opt out of the team before you even arrive – which saves you from having to deal with this kind of underperformer personnel hassle later on.

WRITE A PRE-ARRIVAL MEMO

Before you arrive, people will already be forming an impression of you. Google yourself and see what comes up, because this is exactly what your future team members did when they received the role announcement naming you as newly appointed leader and their new boss.

Perhaps you have a clean history on Google, or perhaps there are untrue stories on the internet. Either way, I advise my clients to take control of what people are saying by writing a pre-arrival memo and sending it via email before starting in the role.

At a minimum, it is very good-mannered and polite to introduce yourself in advance, and say that it is a privilege to be given this opportunity to lead and that you are looking forward to working with them. At a maximum, it offers you an opportunity to control the message regarding who you are, what you stand for and how you intend to tackle the role. You can also use the memo to communicate your working style, and to disclose something personal. Depending on the context, you may or may not wish to state your view yet on what the imminent priorities are. It may be more tactful and more tactical to wait until you have arrived on the ground, and held your one-to-ones with team members.

Sample pre-arrival memo
<insert headshot photo of you>

Hello everyone, I'm Fiona Desmond. As David announced recently, I'm the new Managing Director for the BB Healthcare Division. I am starting on 20 Feb, but thought it might be helpful to introduce myself in advance, acknowledge the great work of the team to date, and lay out what I see as our priorities for FY13.

It's a privilege to be taking on this leadership role. I have been with XYZ company since 1992 and have focused on building a career and reputation in Strategy and Healthcare. For the last five years, I have been serving on the Healthcare Industry Board.

On a more personal level, I am married to Simon with two children, Sarah and Adam. I live in Hampstead in North London.

▶

I play hockey and I like all kinds of sports. Interests outside work help me keep things in perspective and balance.

I would like to congratulate the BB Team on achieving the Industry Award for best new product last year, particularly given the tough competition. This is testimony to your efforts as a team and to the solid leadership of Mike Murphy, whom I would like to personally thank for his support. I recognise that you guys have done a tremendous job already in creating success in difficult conditions, and I acknowledge and appreciate your dedication and your efforts to ensure that we continue on this path.

I look forward to meeting you all soon, and mutually sharing/ listening as together we scope our First 100 Days Team Performance Acceleration Plan. As a brief heads-up, some of the emerging imminent priorities for us – which I will be sense-checking with you – appear to be as follows: reducing operational cost, developing a customer-service ethos for our internal customer, connecting better as a team across all geographies, innovating our products to match consumer concern for the environment, and taking on new stretch missions.

Let me close by saying that I'm looking forward to working with you all this year. See you at the Group Event on 25 Feb, and in the meantime Gina is scheduling a series of one-to-ones and our First 100 Days Team Performance Workshop. My new email address is XXX and mobile is XXXX.

Fiona Desmond

MEET THE TEAM INFORMALLY

It can help put everyone at ease if you give your team the opportunity to get to know you out of the office – and you them – before you officially arrive.

Find or create an opportunity to informally meet the team. For example, depending on the amicability of the situation, your predecessor may be open to inviting you to his leaving

find or create an opportunity to informally meet the team

party. Or perhaps your hiring manager could set up an informal welcome meeting for you prior to your official start date in the role. Meeting the team informally in advance of starting the role is an opportunity for them to get to know you as a 'human being' before experiencing you as the 'task master'. This is your opportunity to present yourself as a person that the team can respect, and like – so don't be scary (!). Be very polite, considerate, and don't boast about how great you are and what fabulous things you achieved in your previous role/previous company as any kind of boasting or posturing can be very off-putting and will only make you seem insecure. Be assured that your reputation will have preceded you.

Let this be about them, not you. Be warm, polite, friendly and open. Smile. Remember people's names. Try to listen more than you speak, but don't appear too distant either. Naturally, given that it is a work occasion, you will inevitably get to hear of the issues and challenges and this can be good added information/ heads up/informal read of what lies ahead.

3 Arrange a swift leadership handover

As I work with clients on how to lead their team in first 100 days, I notice that often one of the first things a newly appointed leader has to do is deal with their predecessor. It is surprising to me that corporations seem reluctant or unable to appropriately manage and handle the situation of what to do with the predecessor, and it is not that unusual if he or she is sitting in your chair in your office when you turn up! It makes for an awkward situation, and no one seems to empower themselves to take charge of how to handle it. You need to step up and handle it yourself because, frankly, there can't be two leaders of the team. The existing team may have residual loyalty to the previous leader, and may continue to take instruction from him/her and not you.

there can't be two leaders of the team

I understand how the predecessor 'fudge' arises. It is usually because there is no new role for the predecessor to go to, perhaps because they are retiring from the company or have been demoted but with no role yet identified. With no place to go (but an understandable desire to still get paid!), the predecessor often offers to help the new guy transition in. This seems sensible in theory, but I have seen many situations at very senior levels where predecessors-with-nowhere-to-go offer to stay around on handover/support for six months. This is too long for any leadership handover, and makes for a totally untenable leadership situation and will undermine your ability to make fast change. Your predecessor will most likely be defensive and resistant to any criticisms or proposed changes you want to make. A disgruntled predecessor may actively work against you by creating coalitions of resistance amongst his loyal supporters, and all in all it is in your best interests, the best interests of the team and your predecessor's best interests if you establish a clean and swift handover.

As part of your preparation phase:

- empower yourself to negotiate a clear finishing date for the predecessor;
- schedule to complete the handover in less than two weeks of you starting;
- arrange for your predecessor to work from home for the rest of his notice period.

You can empower yourself to do this, whilst still being very gracious to your predecessor and handling the person with dignity. My suggestion is that – if not already organised – you set a date for the predecessor's leaving lunch, and at the lunch you publicly thank your predecessor (use the word 'predecessor' as this firmly establishes their new role), thank him or her for staying on to complete the handover, say that the handover will be completed shortly (name the date), and say how pleased you are to be the new leader of the team and you look forward to sharing your plans shortly. Then schedule a team meeting, without inviting your predecessor.

The psychology of using the words 'predecessor', 'handover', 'completion', 'newly appointed leader' and 'new team meeting' all signal that the ending has taken place and a new beginning arisen. Seems overly candid and harsh? It isn't. If you want to succeed as a leader of a team, you have to be an assertive person. As leader you need to own your role, and establish authority sooner rather than later with your new team.

Another situation you may need to be ready to face is when your predecessor stays on as a member of your team, either through demotion or because he had interim reign of your role until your arrival. This person may feel an entitlement to your role, resist a full handover and may resent your arrival. All you can do in this situation is to again be gracious and publicly thank the person in front of the rest of the team, and state very clearly that you are now taking over.

4 Understand the strategic context

Before you start as leader of the team, you should try to understand the strategic context within which your team is required to operate and succeed. You can't start leading your team in a vacuum. There is already a strategic context and timeline, which you need to familiarise yourself with so that the mission for your team is connected into that bigger picture.

> **Understand the strategic context**
> *company vision, strategy, the competition, market dynamics and opportunities, strategic timeline*

At a macro level:

- What is the company vision, mission and strategy?
- What is the CEO agenda?
- Who are the key competitors?
- What are the market dynamics?
- Is this company winning or losing?
- Where are the market opportunities?

What is the strategic timeline?

- What are the critical dates in the future? (e.g. 'two years from now we need to be ready for IPO')

- Is there an immediate crisis? (e.g. 'we need to turn around company fortunes within six months')
- What needs to be done by end of this financial year? (e.g. 'achieve 10 per cent sales uplift on last year')

Sources of information:

- Check out what the company website says (but don't always take it at face value).
- Discuss strategic context with your hiring manager.
- Ask your boss's boss for their perspective on strategy.
- Ideally, meet the group CEO or attend his next roadshow/staff communications event.
- Research the company and the market using detached third-party perspectives via internet searches, analyst reports and relevant industry publications.

Unfortunately, the company strategy and the CEO agenda in some companies are quite difficult to find out, or to understand. Even when the strategy is properly articulated, totally transparent, easy to access and consistently communicated, you might realise that you have been asked to run a team with objectives that are not clearly connected to the company strategy. I don't need to tell you that this does happen within large matrixed multi-site organisations, where strategy is not always joined up.

To succeed as a leader of your team in the first 100 days, seeking clarity on the company strategy will at a minimum set you apart from those 'leaders' who don't bother to even ask the question, and at a maximum will help you to later redefine the role of your team so that it actually does line up more clearly with the company strategy. The more **the more clarity you seek, the more clarity you can bring to your team** clarity you seek, the more clarity you can bring to your team and the faster you will succeed and shine as a leader. Hopefully one day you will be the CEO and then you can ensure that the company strategy is clearly set out and communicated to all employees.

If the strategic context and timeline is not created for you by your bosses, then I suggest you need to be able to create it yourself by choosing a point in the future which represents something to aim for. After all, this is what leadership is all about – the ability and courage to move forward in the face of uncertainty and ambiguity. Pick a time in the future that makes sense for the achievement of strategic goals, and make that your team's compelling strategic context.

5 What is your team mission?

Armed with a greater understanding of the strategic context and timeline, the key question you now need to address is how does your team fit in with, and connect in with, that big picture ambition. You need to be able to see the connection, and a clear line of sight between what you're being asked to do and what the company is trying to achieve and by when. This crystallises the effort of your team, and subsequently crystallises what you will need to achieve with your team in the first 100 days.

> **Understand the strategic context**
> *company vision, strategy, the competition, market dynamics and opportunities, strategic timeline*

> **Set your team mission**
> *clarity on the role and purpose of the team*

Setting your team mission may sound 'simple' enough, but I know that this stuff is not easy. I know that if I popped into any leader's team meeting, at any time, in any company, and asked the team to articulate their team mission, and how it lines up with the company strategy and timeline, I would get as many different answers as there are team members at the meeting. Without clarity on the team mission, there is wasted potential, disjointed effort, increased conflict and missed targets. Without a clear sense of team purpose, little will be achieved and you will have a very lacklustre first 100 days in the role.

CLARIFY, CHALLENGE EXISTING PRECONCEPTIONS ON TEAM MISSION – RESET, REFRAME AND ADD VALUE

Pre-start, take the opportunity of a brand new beginning to sense-check whether the existing team mission is the right one. Have the leadership courage to refresh or totally transform it. Take a view now on the burning platforms, the business case for change. Test your views with your boss. The team mission needs to be a rally cry that will inspire and galvanise the troops into action.

This is an opportunity to do more than replay back what you have heard to date. If you can reframe the mission and role objective in such a way that it already demonstrates your added value, then this is your first and most important role win and you have not yet officially arrived.

don't confuse team targets with the team mission

For example, 'mission' is a word that is often used loosely in corporations. Perhaps you have been told that your team mission is to increase sales by X per cent. But please realise this is simply a team target, not a team mission. A team mission needs to be about thinking bigger, and thinking smarter. An example of a team mission might be to improve customer experience in-store and in the customer care centre – so that resulting increase in sales can occur. By focusing on improving customer experience, perhaps your team will innovate on new products and services that make hitting your sales target easier and faster than if your team had stayed focused on increasing sales of existing products and services.

A crucial aspect of your First 100 Days Team Plan will be your ability to set out the team mission. But it is not the only aspect. Join me in the next chapter and I will explain more about being a mission-setter and about the whole seven-part success formula for your First 100 Days Team Plan.

First100™ Caselet 1

THE LEADER WHO DESTROYED HIS TEAM

A leading financial services firm hired new Operations Director, Marvin, for its Private Wealth Management business. The new leader was an internal promotion and unfortunately proved to be the wrong choice.

Marvin's main problem was his insecurity. He felt threatened by the two members of his team who had applied for his leadership role. Rather than attempt to harness the skills and experience of these direct reports, Marvin decided to move them on. So, within a month of taking on the role, Marvin had dispensed with the two strongest members of his team.

Worse still, by doing so, he lost the respect of the rest of his team, who could see he didn't have the strength of character to get over the fact that other smart people had applied for his role, and felt threatened that they were still around. Three other direct reports abandoned ship in quick succession, demoralised by their new leader's actions. Six weeks into the role, and Marvin had lost five of his most capable direct reports, and was struggling to plug the gaps as word seeped out across the close-knit world of finance that his team was in disarray.

The Private Wealth business began to suffer more broadly as clients moved elsewhere, rather than continue doing business with a firm that did not have its house in order. Less than nine months after his appointment, Marvin moved on (knowing he was about to be asked to go) and the firm had to fight hard to repair both the operational and reputational damage.

The newly appointed leader behaved emotionally rather than rationally, sabotaged his team and his own career progress instead of stepping up and having the confidence and courage to lead a team of strong and capable performers.

The moral of the story

Being the boss is not necessarily about being the 'best' person on the team. You don't need to ever feel threatened by people who are better than you on your team. Consider yourself lucky instead. Having great people around you is a great thing. Delegate more, offload more responsibility to these people and give them the opportunity to shine. The more you help members of your team to shine, the

▶

more you will shine too. People will naturally have more respect for the boss when they play to the strengths of the team members, rather than stifle others for insecure reasons.

Your First 100 Days Team Plan

- First100assist™ Leader–Team Success Formula
- Write your First 100 Days Team Plan

First100assist™ Leader–Team Success Formula

I took the opportunity of writing this book to step back and find a way of packaging up our First100™ experience of leaders and their teams. I distilled all our experience into a seven-part formula for success, to assist you on how to write your optimal plan and tackle the challenge of leading your team in your first 100 days. To successfully lead your team in the first 100 days, you need to lead in seven key ways (see Figure 2.1).

You need to be a:

- Role model
- Mission setter
- Recruiter
- Communicator
- Motivator
- Skills builder
- Target maker

Figure 2.1 First100assist™ Leader–Team Success Formula

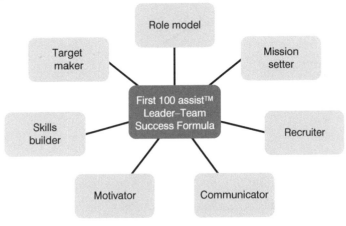

ROLE MODEL

At first, the idea of being a leadership 'role model' may sound a bit odd, a bit pretentious and possibly off-putting to you. Please know that I am not raising it as some kind of clever-sounding idealised theory on how to be a great leader. I am raising it in a very pragmatic way because I want you to realise that in the challenging context of leading a new team in your first 100 days, you have the opportunity to accelerate the performance of the team by setting a higher standard of behaviour and holding others to account to strive for that same standard.

For example, if your standard is that team projects are always delivered 'on time, on budget', guess what starts to happen? Your mantra becomes your team's mantra. Team members soon realise that it is unacceptable to miss deadlines, and 'on time, on budget' becomes part of the team DNA.

As a high-value leader, when you set high standards for yourself and the team, your team members will strive to reach those standards if they want to impress you and stay on your team. Getting your team to strive for a higher standard, is one of the fastest ways of getting your team delivering better and faster results for you.

Strive to be a high-value leader and role model. Start with some good insights and understanding of who you are as a leader, what you stand for:

strive to be a high-value leader and role model

- What are your leadership values?
- What high standards do you set for yourself, and others?
- Are your actions and behaviours consistent with the standards you expect from others?

Develop your list of the high standards you want to set for you and your team:

- What is your standard on time-keeping?
- What is your standard on how team meetings are run?
- What is your standard on level of positivity from the team?
- What is your standard on promoting diversity on the team?
- What is your standard on how people treat each other on the team?

Aspiring to being a great leadership role model means you hold yourself accountable to these high standards, and those around you start to hold themselves accountable to your high standards. The bar is raised, and everybody wins.

Just remember that nobody is perfect, and especially not you. Your team members may not yet meet your standards, and may not always live up to your expectations, but the important point is that you are all trying.

MISSION SETTER

In an earlier chapter, I described the importance of understanding the bigger picture corporate strategic context and defining your team mission within that context. The most important role of a leader with any team in the first 100 days is to be a 'mission setter', i.e. to clarify the role and purpose of the team.

The most essential ingredient of a successful team is a common cause, a unifying mission that everyone agrees on. That's what spurs team members on and drives them to excel. As leader of the team, you need to find and articulate this mission, this common cause, this unifying purpose, this shared vision to which team members aspire to achieve.

Why does this team exist?

A leader and team are only high functioning and 'on task' when they are united on the shared mission, and remain focused on the shared mission. As soon as you have

why does this team exist?

understood the strategic context, the compelling timeline and defined your team mission – only then can you set your team members individual and shared objectives for the first 100 days, and link these to their formal performance appraisals and incentive programmes.

Do not rebuild the team, and then set the mission. Understanding the team's purpose and objective first will allow you to better configure and build a powerful, high-performing team that produces superb results. At the beginning of your first 100 days of leading this team, you need to find and clarify the team mission early on. During your first 100 days of leading this team, the mission enables you and your team to stay focused on what is important. The team mission becomes the stake in the ground, the guiding light, the reminder for why this team exists, the adjudicator of team priorities and resources.

Mission-setting with your team: What is the role and purpose of the team?

- Why does this team exist?
- What are our shared objectives?
- What value are we required to deliver, and to whom?
- Who are our stakeholders, what are their needs, how can we meet their needs?

- If we were designing a team shield or symbol, what would it look like?
- If we had to articulate our team mission in one sentence, what would it be?

Clarifying the role and purpose of the team is about setting a very clear direction for team members. Once the team is very clear on why it exists, then it is easier to prioritise, to strategise and to deliver value and not get distracted or derailed by issues and fire-fighting.

Examples of team mission statements

- **Operations team**
  Our mission is to exceed the expectations of our internal and external stakeholders, by delivering all projects on time, on budget and consistently seeking to improve our processes.

- **Communications team**
  Our team's mission is to help grow our company through creative, efficient and impactful communications initiatives, which safeguard the integrity and value of our brands.

- **IT team**
  Our team exists to propel the company on its path to greater success through harnessing the power of cutting-edge information technology.

- **Customer service team**
  It is our mission to provide all of our hard-won customers with high-quality, responsive and efficient customer care. We continually strive to set the industry standard in customer experience.

> ● **Human resources team**
> *The mission of our team is to provide a positive working environment for all employees and management, maintaining the high levels of morale, efficiency and commercial awareness that define our company.*
>
> ● **Research and development team**
> *We anticipate changing customer needs, and keep our company ahead of the curve with innovations that outstrip the competition.*

RECRUITER

To make maximum impact in your new leadership role, you need to assemble the best possible team in the context of the challenges of this role in order to create an environment where you and everyone around you can succeed.

It goes without saying that in order to achieve great and fast success in the first 100 days of your new role, and beyond, you will need to be able to quickly assemble a great team around you. Given all your earlier preparation work, you should be able to go into your first 100 days with a strong sense of what needs to be achieved in this role, a good understanding of who have you inherited, therefore making it easier to spot the people and skill gaps on the team. You also need to take into account your leadership skill and style, and what that might mean in terms of who you need on your team.

Leader, know yourself:

● What are your strengths?
● What are your limitations?

● What kind of people do you need around you to support your success?

Having a good understanding of your own strengths and weaknesses will help you to make conclusions about the kind of people and skills you need to build around you on your team, and specifically the kind of support you need in the first 100 days. The

understand your own strengths and weaknesses

greater your self-awareness and your self-understanding, the smarter you become at assembling the right team under you. For example, if you are a very expressive person and good on creating the vision, generating ideas and painting the long-term picture but you don't have the patience or numerate capacity to construct the business case for your vision, then these are skills that you can seek to supplement through your team or buy in via consultants.

One of your first steps on recruitment will likely be to figure out the optimal organisation structure and refine your level of direct reports. Ideally your number of direct reports should not exceed 10.

When you recruit your team, consider the following:

● How many key reports do you need? (no more than 10, even if you're the CEO)
● What is the optimal organisation structure?
● Can two roles be collapsed into one?
● What role(s) are missing from the team?
● Do I need a better mix of styles on the team?
● Is there someone from my last organisation that would add value to this team?
● How can HR help me identify new team members internally or externally?

My strong recommendation to you is that you need to be prepared to invest time being a hands-on 'recruiter' in the first 100 days so that you can more easily and speedily figure out the organisation structure and resolve the priority gaps in your team. This is no time to hold back, regardless of HR processes and any 'this is the way we do it here' intransigent bureaucratic timelines. As we all know, there is a war for talent, and to make the greatest impact in your role you will need to find a way to cut through any organisational bureaucracy to quickly and speedily recruit the best people for your team.

Don't let yourself be stymied by HR processes such as waiting for three months to conduct an internal search before allowing an external search to kick off. You have got to be prepared to challenge the recruitment norms in your organisation, and persuade folks that your situation is exceptional. In a war for talent, and given the clear link between having a great team around you and achieving leadership success, you cannot afford to be browbeaten by slow recruitment processes. Remember too that sometimes the very people who are unhelpfully delaying your recruitment processes are the exact same people who later complain that you have not built a strong team around you.

Working with your HR folks, and trusted talent spotters, look inside the organisation for talent and high potentials, and look outside the organisation for people who can bring fresh ideas, a different experience and new market skills to the team. Perhaps you have already ear-marked someone from your previous organisation or department who works in a very complementary way with you, and can help you get a lot of traction early on. However, don't hire previous co-workers as a favour to them or as a comfort blanket for yourself. I have seen this happen and it usually backfires because the team starts to question the leader's judgement.

The lead times on recruitment always end up being longer than anticipated, so you need to start recruitment activities immediately in your first 100 days. Remember to also set up your new recruits for success and empower them to develop their individual First 100 Days Plans.

COMMUNICATOR

You will need to be an effective 'communicator' with your team and team stakeholders in your first 100 days. You could have the best possible team mission and objectives, but if you cannot effectively communicate with your team, and the stakeholders of the team, then very little in the way of progress will be achieved.

The communication gurus always say that even when there is nothing to communicate, you should communicate that **you can never over-communicate** there is nothing to communicate. In other words, you can never over-communicate. The ability to communicate with your team in the first 100 days is very important because it is a very uncertain time for your team members. Being an effective communicator allows you to address your team's concerns and interests and those of your constituent stakeholder.

- ● Team concerns:
  - – What are your plans?
  - – What are we trying to achieve as a team?
  - – What do you expect of me?
  - – How will you know that I am doing a good job?
  - – Will I still have a job by the end of your first 100 days?

- ● Team stakeholder concerns:
  - – Do you understand my needs?

- Can you meet my needs?
- Will we have a productive working relationship?

Get ready to put a team stakeholder communications plan in place:

- Which different groups will the team need to communicate with?
- How frequently?
- What methods will you use to deliver the communication?

Never underestimate the importance of breaking down your high-level messages into more detail to describe what you mean, when you communicate your message. I am reminded of the story of a group of people being told that there is a cat in the next room. The storyteller paused whilst the information sank in, and then he asked each person to describe the cat. Some thought it might be a black and white cat; some visualised a ginger cat; whilst some others wondered if it was a tiger. Perhaps it is an illustrative way of explaining the need to communicate your headline message and fill in the detail. You need to describe in detail what you want, when you want it, what the deliverable might look like.

Being an effective communicator means that the communication has to be two-way. You need to be a good listener as well. The team will have information that helps to enhance your own picture of the current situation, your understanding of the team's stakeholders, how this culture works, who is important in the network. Team members should be allowed to express themselves to you. Communication is not a one-way one-hit event. Being an effective communicator in your first 100 days of leading a team is an ongoing commitment to seek understanding, to share perspectives and to approach conversations via a learning perspective rather than a constant 'tell' perspective. Later on in this book, I shall devote a whole section of Chapter 5 to the topic of 'Communication, communication, communication.'

The elephant in the room

I think that as newly appointed leader of a team, you need to address this question of employee jobs head on. For very good reasons, there may be members of the team who may no longer be required to serve your team. Perhaps they don't have the skills or potential to contribute to fulfilling the team mission. I believe that the fairest message you can send to your team on arrival is to say that everybody on the team will know by the end of 100 days whether or not their job is secure on the team. In other words, you have the guts to openly say that people may be replaced but the process will be as transparent as possible and any uncertainty will end at the end of 100 days. Hopefully, this will settle the team. The high performers realise that they need to impress you, and continue to do a good job and that you will judge them on their merit. The underperformers take it as notice that within three months their fate is sealed. And those people on the fence have an opportunity to up their game and make maximum effort in the next three months.

have the guts to openly say that people may be replaced

MOTIVATOR

To get the highest level of performance from your team in the first 100 days, you need to be able to motivate them to give you 100 per cent of their talent, energy and effort. We all know the difference between simply performing a task, and feeling motivated to perform a task. When we are highly motivated, we will perform the task faster and better than usual. So, if you can be a 'motivator' in your first 100 days, then you will achieve better and faster results from your team.

Motivation is the art of getting other people to do what you want them to do because they want to do it.

Dwight Eisenhower

You need to figure out your first 100 days motivational 'tool kit' to enable you to get the most out of your team members individually and collectively.

To motivate your team, consider the following:

- Use rewards, e.g. pay rise, incentive scheme, promotion prospects, praise.
- Appeal to status needs, e.g. more visibility within the organisation or within the team.
- Recognise achievements, e.g. give 'above average' ranking on exceptional completion of tasks.
- Provide affiliation, e.g. the satisfaction and bond of working closely with others.
- Invest in development, e.g. improve levels of skills and address development areas.
- Offer stimulation, e.g. assign interesting and stimulating new tasks.
- Give independence and responsibility, e.g. more autonomy or task with leading others.

Your approach to motivating your team needs to take into account all of the above, because motivation factors vary across individuals and there is no silver bullet that works for everyone. Believe it or not, some people are not motivated by money. Never underestimate

believe it or not, some people are not motivated by money

how much your team members may be more motivated by the satisfaction they get from working closely with you as a leader that they can admire and respect.

As a thorough checklist, try to cover the following in your first 100 days of leading your team:

- Set challenging and realistic goals.
- Provide fair rewards.
- Give recognition and praise.
- Use feedback and coaching to encourage motivation and performance.
- Give opportunities for visibility within the organisation.
- Encourage some competition.
- Assist with completion of tasks.
- Afford opportunities for team members to work with others.
- Encourage team to develop new skills.
- Provide opportunities for training.
- Give team autonomy regarding task completion.
- Provide positions of responsibility to team members.

SKILLS BUILDER

As leader of your team in the first 100 days, you will need to be a 'skills builder'.

Depending on whether you plan to refresh or radically re-invent the team mission, then your team will need to be up-skilled accordingly. Surprisingly, it can happen (especially with very stressed leaders in their first 100 days) that team members are expected to be able to turn their hand at any task the leaders sets them – and yet this is not logical. Get to know your team and what they can offer. Take into account that the development of your team mission may need to be reined in by what is possible, given the skills of your team or the skills available to you to purchase.

It is unlikely – and not recommended – that you replace your whole inherited team. Usually there is lot of important tacit knowledge and a good mix of skills already available on the inherited team. Replacing the whole team in your first 100 days would only ever be recommended in very exceptional and unusual crisis circumstances.

The key as skills builder is to understand who is good at what and the degree to which your team's skills align to the accelerated achievement of the team mission. One of your quick wins can be to redeploy your people into roles that better play to their skills and talents. Or, for minimal skills investment cost, can you move the dial on achieving maximum performance output? Consider some selective skills investment in particular individuals who you think can radically step up their level of performance.

Build the skills of your team:

- What skills exist on the team?
- What skills are lacking – and will impact on achievement of the team mission?
- What skills, as a leader, can you personally impart quickly to the team?
- What skills-training courses are available in-house?
- What skills will you need to buy – via recruitment or hiring consultants?

- What resources do you have available to invest in training?
- What skills-training would make a massive impact on accelerating team performance?

Take into account both the hard and soft skills necessary for your team to succeed. For example, a 'hard' skill might be a technical skill such as 'market research analysis' and a 'soft skill' might be a more interpersonal skill such as 'stakeholder engagement'.

It can be a very quick win for you with your team if you invest in their skills-building within your first 100 days. It sends out a very strong message that you care about the team's development and that you are interested in their careers. It is a win-win because most people like to build their skills and so it will be of personal motivation and satisfaction to them, and of course their improved skillset is of benefit to you in achieving your goals.

invest in team skills-buildings for a quick win

Ideally, you should set up a process for skills-building throughout the first 100 days of leading this team, such as bringing in a subject-matter expert for half a day two or three times during your first 100 days. With the right brief, two to three targeted skills-building workshops early on can have massive positive effects – as well as improving motivation and skills, it represents an opportunity for team-bonding, and will enable people to transfer and cross-fertilise existing skills and ideas amongst the team.

TARGET MAKER

Your role as 'target maker' is to establish clear targets and measurable results to be achieved by your team by the end of your first 100 days.

Using 'end of the first 100 days' is a way of creating a short sprint deadline for team delivery of early results. It is a device that you can use with your team to set early targets. By creating this 'artificial' deadline for your team, it gives them a timeline to aim for. Even in the face of ambiguity, you can use the end of the first 100 days as a timeline for completing investigations or phase one research – and use it as a decision point on next steps for the rest of your first 12 months in office.

As target maker, you should firstly have a thorough understanding of who are the stakeholders of the team – and who expects the team to deliver what, by when.

- Who are the stakeholders of the team?
  - Who are our key internal customers?
    e.g. my boss, my boss's boss
    e.g. other departmental heads or teams
  - Who are our key external customers?
    e.g. top 10 customers
    e.g. key suppliers
    e.g. regulatory bodies
- Who expects us to deliver what, by when?
  - What are our deliverables?
  - What are the timelines for completing those deliverables?

When you have clarity on key stakeholders and key deliverables, you can set targets for what needs to be delivered by the end of the first 100 days. You can assign each team member to have completed a specific deliverable as per their own area of role responsibility, and you could also create team pods of two or three people who are jointly responsible for completion of cross-area deliverables.

get your team working hard for you

For example, if you are the General Manager of a consumer product set, then by the end of the first 100 days you may require your Finance Director to establish the next 12 months' budget and financial management reporting system, you may require your Marketing Director to submit the 12-month marketing plan, and you may require your Sales Director to submit his strategy for the new sales incentive programme, and so on with other direct reports – but you might also require the Marketing Director and the Sales Director to have collaborated on improving the customer experience in-store.

Get your team working hard for you. Encourage team members to step up and set their own targets. Agree stretch targets, with added bonuses and rewards. Rewards don't always have to be monetary – it could be about celebration, or time off.

As target maker, in the first 100 days, perhaps you can take advantage of the newness of the relationship and team members' desire to impress you, by assigning motivating stretch targets to be completed by the end of the first 100 days. But maintain the right balance on stretch targets and on what is achievable in reality. If you overshoot on stretch versus reality, it can have the opposite effect and immediately de-motivate your team because you are setting them up to fail.

2 Write your First 100 Days Team Plan

Having considered the seven-part formula for leader–team success in your first 100 days, you are now ready to write your First100assist™ Team Plan.

STEP 1: START WITH THE END IN MIND

What do you want to have achieved with your team by the end of your first 100 days?

E.g. My desired outcome is to build a high-performing team by the end of my first 100 days.

There is a great psychology by starting with the end in mind. If you can work out where you want to be in 100 days, then it is like throwing down the gauntlet and fully committing yourself to a future state of success. You are more likely to achieve your goals – or get close to achieving your goals – if you are very clear on what those goals are. By setting out these desired outcomes in a plan, and going public with them with your boss and your team, then it raises the stakes and is like holding yourself to account – further improving your chances of successfully achieving your desired outcome. Make your goals as specific and measurable as possible. If you can assign target values, numbers and percentages, this will give added weight and definition to your desired outcomes.

make your goals as specific and measurable as possible

STEP 2: BREAK DOWN YOUR DESIRED OUTCOME INTO @30, @60 AND @90 MILESTONES

Take your desired outcome on team, and for each leader–team ingredient of success, you need to set out the key sub-outcome, first steps and key monthly outcomes to be achieved within 30-day milestones along the 100 days' journey. Enter these into the First100assist™ Team Plan Template (see page 48).

First100assist™ Team Plan Template

Desired outcome:

SEVEN-PART LEADER-TEAM SUCCESS FORMULA	SUB-OUTCOMES	FIRST STEPS	BY THE END OF 30 DAYS	BY THE END OF 60 DAYS	BY THE END OF 90 DAYS
Role model					
Mission setter					
Recruiter					
Communicator					
Motivator					
Skills builder					
Target maker					

Sub-outcomes

- For each ingredient of success, describe the sub-outcome to be achieved by the end of the 100 days.

- Achieving all the sub-outcomes should equal the achievement of your overall desired outcome.

First-step actions

- For each ingredient of success, what action do you need to take as an immediate first step(s)?

Monthly milestone outcomes

- This is not a list of all the day-to-day activities or actions you need to take. These are the monthly outcomes you want to have achieved by each monthly milestone to know that you are on track to achieving your individual sub-outcome and your overall desired outcome by the end of 100 days.

- For each ingredient of success, describe the monthly milestone outcomes to be achieved @30 days, @60 days, @90 days.

By the end of 30 days

- What would you need to have achieved by the end of 30 days, to know you are on track to achieving your sub-outcome in line with achieving your overall desired outcome by the end of 100 days?

By the end of 60 days

- What would you need to have achieved by the end of 60 days, to know you are on track to achieving your sub-outcome in line with achieving your overall desired outcome by the end of 100 days?

By the end of 90 days

- What would you need to have achieved by the end of 90 days, to know you are on track to achieving your sub-outcome in line with achieving your overall desired outcome by the end of 100 days?

The reason why I recommend that you break down your plan into sub-outcomes, first steps and monthly outcomes is because it is a very useful way of solving the 100-day challenge – by breaking it down into manageable chunks. Plus it means that at each 30-day milestone, you can take some time out and review progress against your plan. Thirty days is enough time to make progress, and keep you on track for achieving your sub-outcomes and overall desired outcome of building a high-performing team by the end of 100 days.

STEP 3: ASSIGN CO-OWNERS TO EACH SECTION OF THE PLAN

the plan offers you and your team an opportunity to put a teaming approach in action

As leader of the team, you can enlist the support of your team members as co-owners of specific parts of the Leader–Team Success Formula – to support you on the optimal delivery of each section of the plan. The plan offers you and your team an opportunity to put a teaming approach in action. With a mechanism of co-owners, there is an immediate opportunity for collaboration, shared ownership and accountability for completion of the plan.

Survey your team members and either ask for volunteers or assign each team member. Play to people's strengths and role functions. For example:

- assign your HR person as your co-owner on 'recruiter';
- assign your marketing person as co-owner on 'communicator';
- assign your sales person as co-owner on 'target maker'.

Make sure that each person on your team has some ownership responsibility and be crystal clear that the co-owner has accountability for delivering that section of the plan, and its sub-outcome, with you from first steps, through to providing updates at the @30, @60, @90 day review milestone team meetings and for final close out at 100 days.

Motivated, high-performing team members will welcome the early opportunity to collaborate directly with you, and show you their expertise and delivery capability. This exercise alone provides you with an important clue on who has a positive mindset and is willing to take up the opportunity of new responsibility and challenges on your team.

STEP 4: SENSE-CHECK AND COMPLETE YOUR TEAM PLAN

When you have filled in the total picture, check to see if you have inadvertently left anything out. Is there anything else that you intended to achieve with your team in the first 100 days?

First100assist™ Team Plan sample

Desired outcome: Build a high-performing team by the end of the first 100 days

LEADER–TEAM SUCCESS FORMULA	SUB-OUTCOMES	FIRST STEPS	BY THE END OF 30 DAYS	BY THE END OF 60 DAYS	BY THE END OF 90 DAYS
Role model Co-owner: John	*Over 75 per cent of my team rate me 'At or above level' on being a great role model.*	Communicate my leadership standards and expectations to the team.	Team standards-setting session held to discuss and agree our high standards and commitments to each other.	Guest speaker invited to talk about expert leadership approaches, with focus on what we can learn/emulate.	Formal feedback session held on quality of leadership performance to date.
Mission setter Co-owner: Garrett	*Our team mission is clearly set out and we are making progress on our goals.*	Understand company strategy, important timelines and existing team mission.	Strategy workshop conducted with my management team. Ideas generated to refresh or radically re-platform the team mission.	New business case developed. Version 1.0 of refreshed team mission socialised with key stakeholders.	New team mission confirmed and agreed. Team performance objectives reset.
Recruiter Co-owner: Fiona	*We have the right people in the right roles.*	Meet team members and take an initial view on quality of the team versus challenges ahead.	Team gaps understood. Executive search underway for key new strategic hires.	Initial team restructure underway. Interviews held for new recruits. Notice given to those who are leaving the team.	Reset roles and responsibilities, and incentive programmes in line with new team mission. Final decisions made on who stays/who goes.

Role	Goal			
Communicator Co-owner: Sarah	*Effective team communications architecture set up and working.*	Schedule team meetings and team events: one-to-ones, weekly team meetings, monthly First 100 Days Workshops.	Each team member met, and their 45-minute presentations conducted.	Blog and Twitter account set up. Town halls / site visits underway.	New e-brochure developed for our suppliers and customers.
Motivator Co-owner: David	*Team members are highly motivated – everyone has stepped up and is delivering results.*	Early ideas gathered on what is most likely to motivate this team to achieve high performance.	Motivation drivers discussed at team meeting. Initial team motivation actions and events agreed.	@60days pulse-check taken on team motivation levels.	Better incentive programmes in place. Regular pulse-check surveys in place for next 12 months.
Skills builder Co-owner: Sophie	*Team members are highly skilled, and/or training plans in place to fill skill gaps.*	Build inventory of necessary skills required to bring this team to high performance.	Skills audit completed – what skills we have, and what skills we lack (hard and soft).	Skills-training workshop held – on the theme of stakeholder engagement.	Skills-training schedule organised for next 12 months.
Target maker Co-owners: Aoibhe, Muireann, Shay.	*First 100 Days team targets achieved.*	Team stakeholders/customers mapped. End of First 100 Day targets and deliverables agreed. Deliverable owners assigned.	@30 Days Team Workshop held – to review progress on First 100 Days team targets and deliverables.	@60 Days Team Workshop held – to review progress on First 100 Days team targets and deliverables.	@90 Days Team Workshop held – to check for final completion of targets and deliverables. New team targets established.

3

@start: Accelerate on arrival

- Launch your First 100 Days Team Plan
- Avoid the leader-as-hero trap
- Bring in 'SWAT team' reinforcements
- Speed up leader–team bonding
- Advice from the executive front line

1 Launch your First 100 Days Team Plan

Hold a First 100 Days Team Plan Workshop with your team within two weeks of starting, letting everyone know that you will be taking this opportunity to share your First 100 Days Team Plan. You can say that you are keen to hear their views on the plan, so that together you can further refine and iterate it.

This will get people's attention and engagement early on. Firstly, it will impress upon them the seriousness of your leadership approach and that you have serious intentions for this team. Secondly, your team will be impressed by your transparency because you are openly sharing your plan. Finally, you are demonstrating inclusiveness by asking for their input.

Table 3.1 Preparing the First 100 Days Team Plan Workshop

PREPPING FOR YOUR FIRST 100 DAYS TEAM PLAN WORKSHOP	NOTES
Schedule a full-day or half-day workshop	Gather together your core team, usually consisting mainly of direct reports and some dotted line reports. This should be approx. 10 or less people. Get everyone physically in the same location, as part of ensuring that you meet everyone on your team in person at least once within your first month.
Consider whether you would like an internal resource or external consultant to facilitate the session	You could run the session yourself, but ideally enlist an experienced facilitator to support you. The role of this person is to run the meeting agenda on time, and ensure that the objective of the session is met and that everyone fully contributes.

PREPPING FOR YOUR FIRST 100 DAYS TEAM PLAN WORKSHOP	NOTES
Set out a clear objective for the session	For example, 'To agree overall priorities and commitments for the team, and to confirm what needs to be achieved by the end of our first 100 days'.
Get ready to share your First 100 Days Team Plan and update it following team input	Share your plan fully so that you can demonstrate leadership transparency early on, and generate discussion. Get fresh input and secure buy-in from the team, to accelerate productive outcomes from the workshop.
Think about who you can assign as a 'co-owner' on each section of the plan	A 'co-owner' is someone on the team who volunteers, or whom you nominate, to support you on the delivery of a specific desired outcome of the team plan.
Consider this to be a leadership role-modelling exercise	By role-modelling your First 100 Days Team Plan and approach, you can create a positive cascading effect by encouraging your team members to run the same approach with their teams.

During your workshop, you will need to touch on each section of the plan. I recommend that you invest particular time and attention on 'mission setter' and 'target maker' – because these are the areas where you need your team to really step up and deliver for you.

ON ROLE MODEL

Explain that the opportunity to lead this team represents a new leadership beginning and that you intend to use the opportunity to strive to continue to improve as a leader. Being a role model is about being an authentic leader, having strong positive values and living those values through your day-to-day behaviour on the job. Describe your leadership style, strengths, weaknesses and development

being a role model is about being an authentic leader

areas. Say that you have high standards and high expectations for yourself and for your team, and that you want to build and lead a high-performing team. Tell them you will be underpinning this aspiration with key leadership actions and key team session activities during the next 100 days. You should also let your team know that you will run formal and informal checkpoints throughout the first 100 days to get their feedback on how you can improve your leadership of this team.

Setting yourself up as aspiring to be a leadership role model may seem like you are putting yourself on a pedestal above the team members, so you need to explain this in an appropriately humble way – by saying that you ASPIRE to be a leadership role model to them and that ultimately they will be the judge as to whether you achieve the title. Opening up a discussion early on about your desire to be a better leader is a great way of setting the bar high for both you and the team.

- Confirm the sub-outcome, first steps, @30/@60/@90 outcomes to be achieved on role model.

ON MISSION SETTER

Set aside sufficient time to discuss the strategic context, important timelines and whether the team mission needs to be radically reset or simply reframed, or refreshed/updated. Listen closely to your team because they will likely have a much better understanding than you of this company or department or function's ability to achieve or implement change. Take note of any fresh views that differ from what you have already heard, and reshape your understanding accordingly. You will have to achieve the team mission together, so you will need to get buy-in from your team.

The fastest way to secure buy-in from your team on the new mission is to get them involved in setting it.

● Confirm the sub-outcome, first steps, @30/@60/@90 outcomes to be achieved on mission setter.

ON RECRUITER

Explain that by the end of the first 100 days, you will have taken a view on everyone's performance and their role on the team going forward. Explain that there may be some changes in personnel required and possibly some new faces coming on board, but that you aim to be as transparent as possible about the changes as early as possible. If there is any information you can share now, then share it. Treat your team members like adults, don't try to sugarcoat a situation when people already know that their job may be at risk.

● Confirm the sub-outcome, first steps, @30/@60/@90 outcomes to be achieved on recruiter.

ON COMMUNICATOR

Ask your team to suggest the style of leadership approach and methods of communication that would work most effectively for this team. Find out if this is a company that embraces new social media as communications tools – and, if not, perhaps this is a differentiator that you and your team can introduce into the company. Be open about your communication style. For example, let people know if you have a tendency to be very candid and explain that its worst manifestation is that under pressure you may come across as very terse – but explain that on the plus side, you are very driven and can make a lot happen for everybody's benefit. Let people know that they can comment

be open about your communication style

on your communication style, on ways to improve it – because you know that it is a key lever in connecting with the team and ensuring the team stays focused on its task.

● Confirm the sub-outcome, first steps, @30/@60/@90 outcomes to be achieved on communicator.

ON MOTIVATOR

Generate some discussion with the team on what motivates them. Highlight the list of motivators, and ask for ideas on how the team can stay motivated throughout the next 100 days. Agree monthly actions that you can jointly take to keep motivation levels high and monthly check-pointing to assess motivation levels.

WHAT IDEAS/ACTIONS CAN WE PUT IN PLACE TO MOTIVATE THIS TEAM OVER THE NEXT 100 DAYS?
Rewards
Status
Achievement and recognition
Affiliation
Development
Stimulation
Independence and responsibility

● Confirm the sub-outcome, first steps, @30/@60/@90 outcomes to be achieved on motivator.

ON SKILLS BUILDER

In the context of the team mission, and end of First 100 Day targets, ask team members if there are known skill gaps in the team.

Get the team to rate itself. For example: as a leadership team, how would we rate our skills out of 10 for:

- ability to set a clear direction (clarity of role, purpose, team mission)?
- ability to bring people with us (our teams, our stakeholders, internal customer, our market)?
- ability to deliver fast results (the technical competence and capability to deliver)?

Check if there are content knowledge gaps on the team, e.g. not up to date on industry trends or technologies. Ask what resources are available to each other on the team or in-house to more quickly and easily skill-share and transfer knowledge across the team.

- Confirm the sub-outcome, first steps, @30/@60/@90 outcomes to be achieved on skills builder.

ON TARGET MAKER

Enlist the help of all team members to map out the key stakeholders/customers of the team. Your team may have more insider information than you, at this stage, on who really matters in this organisation. Get a sense of both the 12-month deliverables and the near-term urgent/crisis deliverables – and take account of both to decide what needs to be completed by the team by the end of the first 100 days. Ideally the team would set their own targets, which you can then review and either agree/refine or add a layer of stretch targets. Ultimately you want your team members to be motivated and high performing, and this means that ideally your role as leader is to guide, direct and fine-tune rather than dictate.

your role as leader is to guide, direct and fine-tune rather than dictate

● Confirm the sub-outcome, first steps, @30/@60/@90 outcomes to be achieved on target maker.

SENSE-CHECK: HAVE YOU INCLUDED ALL URGENT TEAM PRIORITIES, AND EXPECTED DELIVERABLES?

The final question for you and your team at your launch workshop is to ask yourselves whether there is anything not yet recorded on the team plan that needs to be completed by the team in your first 100 days. If there is, make sure that you include these activities within the plan.

For example, are there inherited projects that will continue to need team resources before they can be completed or wound down? The team plan is your opportunity to organise your whole set of team priorities, and manage the workload across monthly milestones – and nothing that requires team time, attention or resources in the first 100 days should be separated out from this plan.

ESTABLISH THE REVIEW MECHANISM FOR THE NEXT 30 DAYS

Leaders are often good at setting a clear direction and delegating responsibilities and tasks to others – which is fine. However, I have noticed that the leader often delegates without any appropriate review or accountability mechanism. You need to put in a system of regular reviews with your team to ensure that when you assign tasks, that you are subsequently updated on progress.

Given that you have not worked with your team members before now, I suggest that in your first 30 days, you take a highly iterative process to communication and delivery of your priority target deliverables. Rather than set out a deliverable and wait for it to be achieved after four or six weeks, you should set out a deliverable and then ask for a weekly update and draft versions every 10 days. You can explain that you are not usually a micro-manager, but that you are deliberating deploying a highly iterative process on key deliverables for the first 30 days until you get a sense of how to work together effectively in the longer term.

WEEKLY UPDATE EMAIL: FROM EACH TEAM MEMBER
✓ PROGRESS
✓ ISSUES
✓ NEXT STEPS

The 'progress' section enables the team member to highlight wins. The 'issues' section is an opportunity to raise concerns and seek help, so that there are no unhelpful surprises later. The 'next steps' section offers a spirit of constant movement forward, onwards and upwards to the next set of actions.

2 Avoid the leader-as-hero trap

On arrival, remember that you are the leader of a team. You are not a lone hero coming to this situation, like Superman arriving on Earth to save the world. By the very definition of the word 'leader', there is a dependency implied that people need to be led – not saved.

you are not a lone hero coming to this situation, like Superman arriving on Earth to save the world

Naturally, as newly appointed leader, you would like to impress your team. We all love being put on a pedestal, and being highly regarded by others. Plus your boss hired you and will want to justify his hiring decision to impress his boss and your team, so it is quite likely that he or she has been talking you up before your arrival. For example, I know of one female executive whose hiring manager either deliberately or mistakenly told everyone she had a business degree from Harvard Business School – when in reality, she had only attended a short executive education course with no exam or resulting qualification.

The team is also in on this leader-as-hero set-up, because they may have been unhappy with their previous leader, and are waiting for you to arrive and save them and show them the way forward. I know of a situation where the whole team thought one of the founders of eBay was arriving to lead their team, when in reality this person had nothing to do with the founding of that company and did a short two-year stint there earlier in her career. And so on, and so forth; the mythology associated with the newly arriving leader starts to grow and spiral even before you set foot in the company.

You want to be a hero, your boss wants you to be a hero and your team wants you to be a hero. When all the temptation points in one direction, then it takes an enlightened person not to fall into this trap. After all, what's the problem?

There are many problems. If the leader is styled as 'the answer', then less attention is paid to building a high-performing team. When the importance of building a high-performing team takes a back seat – it spells disaster in the medium to longer term, and this is not smart. In fact, you are putting too much pressure on yourself to deliver. If you are taking all the pressure on your shoulders to deliver, and playing into a heightened perspective on who you really are, remember that it won't take long for people to realise that you don't have all the answers. Soon enough, the cracks will start to appear and people will be even more disappointed in you if you fall from a pedestal set too high. The higher the pedestal, the greater the fall.

I have seen this all play out in particular with externally joining director level hires. Everyone loves the guy when he arrives, and feels almost privileged that such an 'amazing' person has chosen to join this organisation. Then as soon as he makes a cultural gaffe, or doesn't make the right judgement call on a sensitive issue with team members, people get confused – 'he's amazing, but why did he do that?' – but for a while they still forgive him. One mistake leads to another, and six months into his role appointment, the honeymoon is over and the disillusionment amongst the team and stakeholders is even greater. I know several externally joining director hires hailed as heroes on arrival, that were subsequently fired within the first 12–18 months.

hero behaviours are an arrogance

Hero behaviours are an arrogance. Some leaders can become blind-sided by their own perceived glory, and lose touch with business reality. Yes, you are the chosen one for the new leadership appointment, and you may have a lot of experience but you will not have all the answers, and you need leverage from your team. If you pitch up, and play into this role of leader-as-hero, it is an illusion and will put you under too much pressure. Better for you if you calibrate your role correctly and ensure there is a balanced emphasis on what you and your team are going to achieve in the first 100 days. Instead of going the solo leader-as-hero route, you can achieve better and faster output in your first 100 days and beyond if you harness the skills, efforts and energy of a multiple number of people around you.

The 'hero' is a lone person, a lone ranger, self-oriented – great in a one-off crisis moment – but not as effective as a long-term strategy as someone who has galvanised an army of followers and maximised output and productivity in service of a shared goal over the short, medium and long term.

Much better if the leader is not self-styled or styled by others as 'hero' but remembers, with humility, that he or she cannot achieve much in the long run without the support of the team. Focus your efforts on being an authentic leader, a leadership role model, a person who is comfortable within their own role skin – rather than some imaginary superhero version of yourself.

3 Bring in 'SWAT team' reinforcements

I like to find ways for my clients to accelerate their leadership and team performance in the first 100 days, but my SWAT team reinforcements suggestion needs to be handled with care. It makes sense that if you bring in some extra expert resources for this temporary transition phase, then more results will be achieved earlier and faster. However, if the SWAT team concept is not properly communicated or correctly positioned, be aware that you might alienate members of your team who might resent you for bringing in external resources to work with them on what they might consider lies within their existing capability.

On arrival, you can do some quick sense-checking with your boss, and key team members, in order to understand the context and sensitivities – and budget – regarding bringing in external resources. Notwithstanding the nuances of carefully managing internal sensitivities, if at all possible, I recommend you go for it in terms of accessing temporary expertise to accelerate the performance of your team – not least because bringing in outside help will quickly shake up any insular behaviour in the group and demonstrate that you are serious about changing the status quo.

Empower yourself to hire in extra help if you want to fast-forward priority team activity. The beauty of the first 100 days is that it is a very short time period, and external consultants can be given a very specific brief and very specific deliverables to be completed within a clear sightline of the end of your first 100 days.

Also, take advantage of being the new guy. The stakes are high. Everyone is pleased that you have arrived, and they are keen to make a good impression on you. Your boss wants you to succeed and your first 100 days is a window of opportunity to get more budget from your boss than at any other time in your role appointment.

take advantage of being the new guy

Consider hiring in the following resources as part of your 'SWAT team' of reinforcements to accelerate activities with your team in the first 100 days.

- *First100™ consultant*:

  A specialist on the 'first 100 days' who can support you and your team to have an accelerated first 100 days performance by assisting you on how to write your optimal First 100 Days Team Plan, by supporting you on running team workshops, and by keeping you and your team accountable for delivery of the First 100 Days Team Plan.

- *Executive search consultant*:

  To accelerate recruitment for priority vacancies that you identify on your team, you may want to brief an external head-hunter rather than rely on the internal pool or your personal network alone to find new strategic hires.

● *Strategy consultant:*

Depending on your strategic ability, the seniority of the role you are hired to complete, your access to budget for consultants and the quality of strategic thinking on your team, you could consider hiring a strategy consultant/ team to support you on developing your vision, strategy and team mission.

● *Finance analyst/consultant:*

Being new to role, you should have a lot of questions about the financials and relevant metrics pertaining to your role, organisation, market and industry. If these numbers are not ready available or require some research/data gathering, then it makes sense that you hire in a finance analyst and brief this person to work with your team to gather answers to your questions. This needs to be a very numerate person, good on spreadsheets and business case manipulation – but not necessarily a very senior or expensive person.

Ideally, these suggested resources should not stay for longer than your first 100 days. If that is clearly explained to your team, then you will have less resistance to team members who may feel threatened by 'outsiders' coming in to work alongside you and them.

4 Speed up leader–team bonding

As time passes, you and your team will eventually bond. You begin to trust them, they begin to trust you. For example, a candid remark by you is not taken so personally when team members eventually realise that you are candid with everyone. So you could just wait for time to elapse whilst everyone gets to know each other and feel comfortable working together. Or you can consciously try to speed up the leader–team bonding process in the next 100 days, in the pursuit of faster outcomes. The faster the bond grows between leader and team, the more accelerated the leader–team performance will be against plan.

The fastest way to break down barriers and build trust between you as leader and your team is quite simply down to your leadership behaviours, and how you treat people day to day from the moment you arrive. Don't underestimate the importance of being a good person, as well as a **if your people can relate to you, respect you and like you, they will work harder for you** good business person. If your people can relate to you, respect you and like you, they will work harder for you.

There is a difference between getting people to like you, and getting people to respect you. Too many newly appointed executives focus on the former – whereas it is more important in a work context that people first respect you and the value you bring as leader of the team. In any case, team members don't have to like you, but it certainly helps if they do – because as humans we go out of our way for people we like. To put it another way, you don't need to establish yourself as everybody's new best friend, but don't try to alienate people either.

To speed up the leader–team bonding process in your first 100 days, pay particular attention to deliberately demonstrating the following behaviours:

- Be straightforward.
- Demonstrate fairness.
- Ask for help.
- Be friendly.
- Be optimistic.
- Deliver early value.

The obvious 'don'ts' are as follows:

- Don't lose your temper.
- Don't say anything politically incorrect.
- Don't tell jokes, in case you inadvertently offend someone.
- Stop saying how great your last company was.
- Stop saying 'you' to the team, and start saying 'we'.

Walk the floor as much as possible with your team, on arrival. In a traditional sense, this meant literally walking the factory floor. But in a modern sense, this means taking the time out for informal touch-points such as lunch or travel time to check in with your team on how things are going, what are the bottlenecks, how can you help. The leader–team bonding process speeds up when people make a connection with you and this happens a lot faster when people meet in person.

First100™ Caselet 2

THE LEADER WHO WANTED TO BE FRIENDS WITH HER TEAM

Before Karen took on the role of Chief Marketing Officer at a rival technology company, she spent three months on 'garden' leave. By the time she arrived for her first day, her team had been without a leader for almost five months. The anticipation of her arrival grew.

Everyone was relieved when Karen finally arrived. Plus she seemed so friendly and nice, and fun!

Karen was keen to make a good impression, wanted everyone to like her and was not comfortable being an authoritative boss. She avoided giving direct orders and tried to be a friend instead of a leader to her direct reports. One hundred days later, the atmosphere in the office was fun and lively, but there was no clear strategy set out. Team members started taking liberties and relaxed their approach to deliverables and deadlines. Karen realised that the team was taking advantage of her 'good nature' but she struggled to assert herself, and it felt too late to start behaving like a boss. Team communication was unstructured, sporadic and reactive. Everyone liked working on Karen's team, but no one respected her as leader of the team. No one was in charge, the team started to get a bad reputation in the company, and within six months Karen's boss realised that this was now an even worse situation than prior to Karen's arrival.

Under pressure from her boss to get the team back on track, Karen belatedly enlisted support from an internal mentor, who advised her she had no time to waste in re-asserting herself as leader of the team. Her mentor made it clear that Karen had to provide her key reports with structure and clarity. Karen needed to develop a team plan, improve team communication and get results fast.

▶

Karen eventually managed to turn the situation around by the end of the year – but it was even more difficult to re-assert herself with her team after six months, than it would have been if she had got off to the right leadership start from day one.

The moral of the story

This team was leaderless for five months, and the team remained leaderless for the next six months after Karen arrived. Karen may have been appointed as leader of the team, but she never truly showed up until her job was at risk. For sure, be friendly with the team, but don't try to be friends with the team. As leader you need to take charge, and direct the team's activities and priorities. Some leadership decisions will make you unpopular with the team, and if that bothers you then you may be in the wrong job.

5 Advice from the executive front line

Taking time to make sure you have the right people in the right roles to drive success is one of the areas I focused on after my first month arriving in the UK.

I started a series of informal dinners with my direct reports and their immediate top teams – known as the Egg Timer dinners. Early in the evening, in the private dining room of a local restaurant we gathered for dinner. Each person got three minutes (we used an egg timer to make sure they stuck to this) to share their background, some info on their family, what they did outside work, etc. That immediately broke the ice and it always amazed me that their colleagues often didn't know this information. Then I gave each person the opportunity to be CEO for 10 minutes, to pitch to their colleagues and I on how they'd run the company if they were the new CEO. This covered where they'd invest, what they'd cut back on and how they'd deliver revenue and profit. The ideas and discussions gave me a real sense of the capability, quality and courage in the talent around me and where the natural biases lay. I did over 10 of these dinners, three per week and so in a few weeks I'd covered the top 100 execs in the company.

Guy Laurence, CEO, Vodafone UK

To make a real impact in the first 100 days you need two things: proper transition support and a clear agenda.

Andrew Wright, Director of Leadership and Partner Development, Ernst & Young

Show your human side and be yourself. This can allow you to build support very quickly.

Olaf Swantee, CEO, Everything Everywhere

In the first 100 days, the greatest challenge is understanding who and what is important. Recognise that those who shout the loudest may not be the ones you should be spending time with.

Luis Alvarez, President, EMEA and Latin America, BT Global Services

In the first 100 days you need to quickly build an understanding of your stakeholders and their dynamics.

Guy Warren, Chief Operating Officer, FTSE Group

New-to-role leaders from outside should spend one to two days in the business before they officially begin their role. This time should be spent absorbing as much as possible about who your people are, their working styles and the types of behaviour they exhibit.

Peter George, CEO, Clinigen

In your first 100 days it's important to strike a balance between understanding the new organisational context you find yourself in, delivering some early wins and getting to know your team and the people around you.

Dan Dobson-Smith, Director of Organisational Development, Sony Music Entertainment

Effective leaders create a vision for the future that's compelling and achievable and then put the resources in place to deliver that vision. From a personal perspective, the most important thing for a person in a leadership role for the first time is to set an example by displaying total commitment and passion for what they want the business to achieve.

Paul McElvaney, Founder, Learning Pool

Ensure you show an appreciation of whom and what has gone before you. Gain a deep understanding of the culture of your team in the context of the wider organisation and always be conscious of how you may be perceived.

Lisa Williams, Managing Director, John Lewis (HW)

Executing an acquisition means that leaders in their first 100 days need to live up to their company's cultural principles without fear of bringing in new ideas.

Lance Uggla, CEO, Markit

Make a decision and then make that decision right.

Magnus Djaba, CEO, Saatchi & Saatchi UK

The most pressing challenge facing new leaders is filling the credibility gap. Early results need to be delivered, and the first 100 days need to be handled with composure so key stakeholders perceive you as a leader of substance.

Bob Fuller, Director, Fixnetix

Don't be afraid of your 'newness', it is the newness of your perspective that is valuable.

Ian Phillips, Co-Founder & Director, CO_2 DeepStore

part two

Middle

@30 days: Optimise team performance

- Review progress against team plan
- Spot dysfunctional group behaviours
- Capitalise on the strengths of the team
- Update your First 100 Days Team Plan
- Advice from the executive front line

1 Review progress against team plan

You can keep the team plan on track by conducting thorough progress reviews of the First 100 Days Team Plan with your team at the key milestones of @30 days, @60 days and @90 days.

The @30 days milestone is the first major pause and opportunity to review team progress against your First 100 Days Team Plan.

Don't underestimate the opportunity to also use the @30 Days Team Workshop to facilitate the acceleration of the all-important working and social bond between leader and team, and amongst the team itself.

Review progress against First 100 Days Team Plan

@30 DAYS TEAM WORKSHOP

1 Review your First 100 Days Team Plan.

2 Are you and your team on track to achieve the 30-day milestones set out in the plan?

3 Are you and your team where you expected to be @30 days?

4 Take stock of what is working well/not well with your team plan @30 days:
   - What more can you and the team do to improve performance against plan?
   - Brainstorm solutions to any blocks/challenges.
   - Think about the performance acceleration opportunities.
   - Who can help you and the team with this exercise, and act as your sounding board/advisor?

In your first 30 days, reviewing progress should have represented a large portion of your time with your team. It doesn't mean that you were 'doing' the tasks, but it should mean that you were keeping check on whether the tasks you assigned to team members were progressing or not – and this enabled you to step in to support, or to re-assign tasks accordingly.

The @30 Days Team Workshop is a good opportunity to review team progress against plan, set the tone early on, and establish an effective and safe place for issue resolution and problem-solving.

Top tips for @30 Days Team Workshop:

- Establish team meeting ground rules, to send signals regarding meeting importance and focus.

  Top tip: insist that all phones/laptops/devices are turned off during team meetings.

- Check that everybody is contributing. Introverts are likely to wait to be asked to contribute.

  Top tip: ask quiet members to express their views.

- Don't overly dominate the meeting. Play a more participative mode, to allow others to shine.

  Top tip: let someone else on the team run the meeting.

- Pay attention to misbehaviour, such as talking over each other/interrupting each other.

  Top tip: use humour to call out misbehaviours.

- Encourage diverse views.

  Top tip: appoint someone as devil's advocate, to stimulate debate/opposite thinking.

- Let the team know that conflict is okay.

  Top tip: state openly at the beginning of the meeting that you want to hear everybody's opinions, that team meetings are an opportunity to debate differences of opinion.

- Be optimistic. Don't let team meetings spiral into negative despair about all the problems.

  Top tip: train people to talk about solutions as well as problems.

And when the going gets tough:

- Hold people to account, but never be derogatory, demeaning or attacking.

  Top tip: focus on problem-solving.

2 Spot dysfunctional group behaviours

You have been working with your team for a month, and it is important that you can quickly spot when the team is high-functioning or not. Bion's Theory of Groups describes how a work group (team) is functional and effective when it stays focused on the primary task of the group, i.e. what the group has formed to accomplish. The most helpful aspect about understanding and applying this 'staying on task' mindset is that it forces you to define what the task is. I would argue that in your first 100 days, your team is only *on task* when the team is performing activity in service of the First 100 Days Team Plan.

Get in the habit of sense-checking whether the task has been clearly stated prior to a team meeting. During the meeting, get in the habit of sense-checking whether or not you and the team are 'on task'. Develop a crystal-clear awareness on whether the team is focused on its objectives or too inclined to get side-tracked.

Are we on task?

get in the habit of sense-checking whether or not you and the team are 'on task'

- What is the task of this team meeting, i.e. What is our objective?
- Is this meeting on task?
- Is this discussion on task?
- Is this team staying on task?
- When does the team go off task? And why?

'Are we on task?' is a simple but powerful sense-checking question to ask at any point, as a way of staying focused. Try it at your next meeting. It forces you to be very clear about the objective of the meeting, and to ensure that you stay on task by staying focused on achieving the objective of the meeting.

For example, in a sales team meeting, ask why does the team constantly discuss manufacturing issues or spend 20 minutes criticising marketing efforts, when we should be talking about sales methods? Remind everybody that the objective of the meeting was to reset sales targets. Be aware that the team has gone off task for a reason. It is easier to complain about manufacturing and marketing than it is to take responsibility for not meeting sales targets. By getting into the 'on task' mindset, you will start to become more aware of why people go off task, and your job as leader is to get them back on track.

Dysfunctional behaviour occurs when the team goes off task. Bion's Theory of Groups (1961) describes three scenarios when a group/team can go off task – a behavioural manifestation of the anxiety of the work group. Bion calls these 'Basic Assumptions' (dependency, fight or flight, pairing). In 1974, Turquet added a fourth basic assumption called 'one-ness'. A further fifth basic assumption ('me-ness') was developed by Lawrence, Bain and Gould (1996). Bion says that Basic Assumptions occur when the group/team are anxious and get distracted from focusing on the primary task, i.e. the group goes off task. Inspired by current examples of basic assumptions, and using First 100 Days as the context, let me attempt to apply these theories to assist you on how to spot dysfunctional behaviours in your team in your first 100 days.

DEPENDENCY

This group dysfunction occurs when the group disempowers itself by handing over all its dependence and power to its newly appointed leader, as if it has nothing to contribute and is just **you need to empower your team to deliver** waiting for instructions on what to do. You want your team to be high-performing, and that means you must empower your team members to make progress and make decisions without having to get your permission all of the time. To lead a high-performing team, you need to agree on the outcomes to be achieved and then empower your team to deliver – not micro-manage your team on how every action is achieved.

- ● *@30 days checkpoint:* Is your team overly dependent on you, or quite good at self-managing?

FIGHT OR FLIGHT

This group dysfunction occurs when the group is constantly poised to flee from the task. If your team members are easily distracted by minor issues or prefer to avoid tasks completely, then for sure the team is not high-performing. As leader of the team, try to notice whether your team is good at staying focused on what they need to do, or whether they are constantly poised/susceptible to going off task and getting involved in other activities rather than face their particular task challenges. Call them on it, point out the behaviour so that the team becomes more self-aware and changes its behaviour. A good example of this would be if the team members find excuses to delay, reschedule or not attend your @30 Days Team Plan Workshop. I would also be keen to flee the workshop if I had not made any progress with my area of responsibility.

- ● *@30 days checkpoint:* Is your team easily distracted, and too inclined to flee the task?

PAIRING

This group dysfunction occurs when the whole team unconsciously places all their hopes in a pair of people within the group as if this pair will 'save the day'. This behaviour manifests itself by two people taking over the meeting or taking over the group, and the group allowing this to happen. As leader of the team, it is more likely that you will dominate the group and you might unwittingly develop an intense relationship with a number two/right-hand person on your team and before long the rest of the team just hands over their power to the two of you. Don't allow this to happen. Each member of your team needs to contribute and participate in team progress.

- ● *@30 days checkpoint:* Is the team overly reliant on two people to save the whole team?

ONE-NESS

This group dysfunction occurs when the group agrees on everything and there is no challenge allowed within the group. A

there should always be a healthy amount of conflict in any group

cult would be a good example of the one-ness basic assumption. As leader of your team, you want to create an overall sense of harmony and positive working relationships, but you also need to allow members to challenge/debate/disagree and have conflicts

with each other and with you. There should always be a healthy amount of conflict in any group, for it to continue to challenge and renew itself in the face of new issues and decisions to be taken.

- ● *@30 days checkpoint:* Is your team separating itself from the rest of the organisation and acting like it is an elite group with all the answers?

ME-NESS

This group dysfunction occurs when the individual goals are more important than the team goals. You can spot this when a team member is serving only his interests or his department interests without taking into account the needs of the rest of the group. As leader of the team you need to ensure that this group is encouraged to behave like a team with mutually beneficial goals, and not end up with a dysfunctional group of self-serving individuals.

- ● *@30 days checkpoint:* Is your team acting like a team or just a bunch of individuals serving their own interests ahead of the shared interests of the team?

As the leader of the team, it will be very interesting for you to become more aware of all these types of group dysfunctions because this unconscious behaviour happens all the time in work groups. If you can consciously look out for it and spot it, then call it out and it will make you the smartest person in the room. As leader of the team, you want to be seen to be the smartest person in the room from time to time!

you want to be seen to be the smartest person in the room from time to time!

There is another basic assumption not covered by Bion, nor others, which I have spotted – and coined – in the context of the first 100 days of leading a team:

'SUBVERSION'

This occurs when the nominated leader has been subverted by the team. Ask yourself, who is the boss of this team? Are you sure it is you?

I have noticed a leader–team group dysfunction that often arises in the first 100 days of leading a team. By virtue of being new, the leader is somewhat vulnerable in their first 100 days until they establish themselves and feel fully secure. During that period of vulnerability, other people on the team and their strong influences can come in to play.

An example is when the team overwhelms the leader, and the tail starts wagging the dog. By that I mean that the team uses its knowledge base as power, and starts to tell the leader what to do, rather than the other way around. The leader is dealing with so much, that they are unconsciously subverted and abdicate responsibility on decision-making to team members without checking in with what is really going on.

Another subversion example is when a member of the team tries to take advantage of the leader's newness to further their own agenda. Sometimes this background person is a force for good, but other times it is a very charming individual who is effectively preying on the newly appointed leader's insecurities to further their own individual power and politics agenda. The newly appointed leader has a lot to deal with, and may willingly accept the influence without realising that a power grab is taking place.

So, ask yourself, is there someone in your leadership life, secretly (or not even secretly) in charge of you? And more importantly, what are you going to do about it to take back control?

- *Is it your HR person?*

  Is your HR person overly influencing your perception of people and pace, and how to get things done here? Are you overly reliant on your HR person to make decisions on the people in your team?
  - Are you in charge of your HR person, or is your HR person is in charge of you?

- *Is it your personal assistant?*

  Is your PA too bossy, power-tripping and overstepping the mark on running your diary?

  Are you overly confiding in your PA, and overly concerned with your PA's opinion on everything and everyone?
  - Are you in charge of your PA, or is your PA in charge of you?

- *Is it your new 'buddy'?*

  Has someone very quickly and easily ingratiated themselves with you to the extent that you can no longer function effectively without them? Are you relying too

much on one member of your team? You have only known these team members for 30 days, but do you find yourself in some kind of inseparable 'new best friend' attachment with someone on the team?
 - Are you in charge of your new buddy, or is your new buddy in charge of you?

Take back control

Assert yourself as the leader of the team. With some teams, it may be a constant battle to assert yourself as the leader in the beginning, especially

assert yourself as the leader of the team

if you have very strong and opinionated members on your team. You have to stay in control. Remember your job is not to get people to like you. You are not friends with your team members. You are their boss. Be the boss.

3 Capitalise on the strengths of the team

Another smart approach to accelerating the performance of your team in the first 30 days is to quickly identify and capitalise on the natural strengths of the team. If you can harness the existing natural strengths of the team early on, then you will deliver results faster. By delivering quicker results, you will impress your stakeholders, build confidence and can potentially secure more budget and more resources early on – which allows you to strengthen your position and continue to deliver even more results in the future. It is all about creating a positive momentum as fast as possible, and then creating a positive spiral of events.

By now, you will have the hands-on experience of working with and interacting with your team members for a month and that is sufficient time to reflect on the key strengths of the team.

WHO IS THE STRATEGIC THINKER, THE CHANGE AGENT, THE EXECUTOR?

Think about how team members have responded to a new beginning, and see who has stepped up naturally as a strategic thinker, or as a change agent or as an executor.

Figure 4.1 Identifying natural strengths

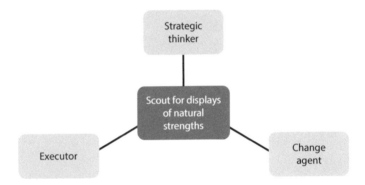

- The 'strategic thinker' is the person on your team who sees the big picture, spots patterns, is insightful and future-facing. This person can support you on setting a clear direction, aligned to team mission and desired outcomes of the First 100 Days Team Plan. As time goes by, it is easy for the team to get derailed and lose focus from the plan. At the 30-day milestone, and at each milestone beyond, the strategic thinker can assist you on reminding everybody on clarity of direction, and not veering off course.

- The 'change agent' is the person who has strong influence within the team. This person is already naturally motivated to deliver the go-forward First 100 Days Team

Plan, and can assist you on bringing people with you. You need people on your side, within the ranks, who can galvanise others. The less resistance to change, the faster you guys can deliver on the plan.

- The 'executor' is someone very driven to get results. This person knows how to run a process, and ensure that everyone delivers on time and on budget, according to the First 100 Days Team Plan. Some teams are busy, and productive, but continuously circle back and can't quite make the deadline. What you need on your team is someone who makes sure that deadlines are adhered to, so that your First 100 Days Team Plan brings in results by the end of the 100 days.

Don't just look in the obvious places for these kinds of strengths. The strategic thinker may not necessarily be in a strategic role. Sometimes it is the introvert in the corner who has **pro-actively seek out the strengths within your team** paid attention to everything but has not yet been asked his opinion. In your first 100 days, you have the opportunity to come to this group with fresh eyes. Give everybody a chance. Pro-actively seek out the strengths within your team.

Be alert to spotting these kinds of strengths and potential amongst your people. If you are fortunate enough to have people with each of these strengths on the team, then capitalise on them as soon as possible by giving these people responsibilities that more deliberately play to their strengths. This will accelerate your team's performance in the first 100 days. Involve the strategic thinker on the big picture and future planning. Enlist the change agent on influencing others and galvanising the team forward. Give the executor responsibility for ensuring that everyone delivers according to the timeline of the First 100 Days Team Plan.

If you don't have these kinds of strengths on your team, then it follows that you are at a disadvantage when it comes to achieving high performance. During your recruitment processes, keep in mind how you may be able to bring in technical skills required plus fill any missing gaps on strategic thinker, change agent and executor.

WHAT PASSIONS ALREADY EXIST ON THE TEAM?

If you can spot what passions exist within the team, then these are the areas where people will be already naturally motivated to work harder and more easily disposed to working harder for you. For example, if the team reports to the CTO (Chief Technology Officer) it is quite likely that some team members have a strong passion for investigating and developing new technologies. The CTO could set up a process, such as 'fortnightly innovations Friday', when team members can take the morning off from day-to-day tasks and meet as a group to research new technologies that would transform the way this company does business, through better information and insight gathering. By enabling team members to unleash their passion for new technologies, you may gain a reputation as a team for ground-breaking innovations.

AM I ALLOWING EACH PERSON THE OPPORTUNITY TO PLAY TO THEIR NATURAL STRENGTHS?

Don't let anyone off the hook. Everyone has natural strengths – you just need to identify them and play to them. When your review progress against your First 100 Days Team Plan, check if you have correctly assigned tasks that play to the natural strengths of team members. You could divide up sections of the plan, depending on individual strengths. For example, whoever is a good communicator could be charged with publicising the plan and sharing with key stakeholders. The best organiser in the group could be charged with governing the plan because of their organisational skills. Your expressive people could be tasked with running cross-team think-tanks, idea-generation and creative activities. Are your numbers people writing business cases? For the sake of

everyone has natural strengths – you just need to identify them and play to them

progress, perhaps you could take some tasks off underperformers. For example, if there are team members who have been given notice to leave, then they are unlikely to be giving 100 per cent effort at this stage.

At First100™, we worked with a team in which one member was financially aware and he became the 'tutor' for the team in simplifying the financial language so everyone could understand it. In another client, there was a new member of the team who needed to get up to speed quickly, and a team member whose strength was specialist knowledge agreed to provide deep-dive tutoring and run knowledge-sharing sessions for the new guy and anyone else interested in attending.

4 Update your First 100 Days Team Plan

As a final part of your @30 Days Team Workshop, the team need to refresh and reset the next 30 days' actions.

The rigour and discipline of updating your First 100 Days Team Plan at monthly milestones will reap significant benefits for you:

● The team stays focused on what really matters.

- Each element of the seven-part formula for team success is thoroughly considered and kept top of mind.
- The team is motivated by coming together and tracking its own performance.
- Team members share the experience of solving problems together.
- Any early issues are ironed out and resolved, in an appropriate forum.
- A clear direction is reset for the next 30 days.

Update First 100 Days Team Plan

AT THE END OF YOUR @30 DAYS TEAM WORKSHOP

Refresh and reset the actions for the next 30 days, based on your first 30 days' experience, and on:

- a review of progress against the First 100 Days Team Plan;
- performance acceleration tactics on how to spot and correct group dysfunctions;
- performance acceleration tactics on how to capitalise on the strengths of the team.

---

5 Advice from the executive front line

Empower your people – the successful leader is the one who can delegate most effectively.

James Ryding, Director of International Talent Acquisition, NBC Universal

Realise that what truly motivates people is a sense of fairness. Show that you are not too prescriptive and that you will judge your people on results.

Stuart Woollard, Director, Management Learning Board, King's College London

Give direct reports a special project to work on early on that is suited to their skillset. Allow them to develop confidence under you by playing to their strengths.

Pontus Noren, Founder and CEO, Cloudreach

By this point [one month in] you should have a keen understanding of what makes the business tick.

Kate Griffiths-Lambeth, Global Head of Human Resources, Stonehage

Come to understand you team's behaviour, what drives this behaviour, and call people on behaviour that doesn't fit with your vision for the team.

Clare Martin, Director of Customer Experience, Daisy Communications

You need to check in emotionally and assess where your people are. It's essential to be able to observe any resentments around your appointment, and address these, as they can form an obstacle to leadership success.

John Buekers, VP of HR EMEA, Hitachi Data Systems

Be very open about who you are and what you bring as a leader. You will then quickly get a sense of the personalities and functional competence present in your team. You have to be seen to be genuine in your desire to make a difference.

Denis O'Flynn, Managing Director, Pernod Ricard UK

Come in with an open mind and try and see the reality behind the rhetoric. Pay attention to how your direct reports relate to one another just as much as to how they relate to you.

Jean Harrison, Director of Human Resources, University of Westminster

Where many failures occur in a leadership transition is when a new leader neglects to take the time to get to know and utilise the knowledge of their team.

Judy Goldberg, Director of International Learning and Development, Discovery Communications

5

@60 days: Sustain a strong momentum

- Review progress against team plan
- Remove barriers to high performance
- Communication, communication, communication
- Update your First 100 Days Team Plan
- Advice from the executive front line

1 Review progress against team plan

You can keep the team plan on track by conducting thorough progress reviews of the First 100 Days Team Plan with your team at the key milestones of @30 days, @60 days and @90 days.

The @60 days milestone is the second major pause and opportunity to review team progress against your First 100 Days Team Plan. By now, you and your team will be seeing results coming through, and this progress review will serve to energise everyone for the final phase of the plan.

Don't underestimate the opportunity to also use the @60 Days Team Workshop to facilitate the acceleration of the all-important working and social bond between leader and team, and amongst the team itself.

Review progress against First 100 Days Team Plan

@60 DAYS TEAM WORKSHOP

1 Review your First 100 Days Team Plan.

2 Are you and your team on track to achieve the 60-day milestones set out in the plan?

3 Are you and your team where you expected to be @60 days?

4 Take stock of what is working well/not well with your team plan @60 days:
   - What more can you and the team do to improve performance against plan?

- Brainstorm solutions to any blocks/challenges.
- Think about the performance acceleration opportunities.
- Who can help you and the team with this exercise, and act as your sounding board/advisor?

At this point, you are well and truly underway with your team and your First 100 Days Team Plan. Sometimes leaders find it may even be tempting to abandon the @60 Days Team Workshop, as their confidence grows and they feel more secure with their team and what needs to be done. However, I urge you to stay focused on the review process and stay with the process until the end of the 100 days.

The @60 Days Team Workshop is a good opportunity to review progress, facilitate team bonding and to encourage the development of positive cultural norms within the team.

Top tips for @60 Days Team Workshop:

- Use it as a pressure valve release mechanism.

  Top tip: have a 'check in' at the beginning of the meeting to ask how everyone is doing.

  Top tip: ensure the agenda is not too tightly squeezed, so that there is sufficient time for everyone on the team to raise issues that may be frustrating, and that together the team can help resolve.

- Use it as an opportunity for team bonding/social interaction.

  Top tip: hold the meeting off-site, and include sufficient time for team lunch to get to know each other away from group tasks.

- Signal your commitment and willingness to invest in the team's development.

  Top tip: bring in an external speaker, such as a business book author or skilled specialist for a pertinent 60–90 minutes' learning injection.

- Update the team on high-level company strategy or new CEO priorities.

  Top tip: don't just stay at the level of your own team's mission and tasks. Remind everybody about the bigger picture and the company's strategic journey.

- Raise the issue of how to better address the team's stakeholders' concerns and interests.

  Top tip: take some time out to run a temperature check on the level of stakeholder engagement. Consider inviting a stakeholder to the session to advise on team plans.

- Find out more about your organisation.

  Top tip: ask your team for more information about the culture and politics within the organisation.

- Demonstrate your openness and loyalty to the team.

  Top tip: if you can disclose something confidential to the team in a managed risk way, then you are signalling that you trust the team and you will benefit from reciprocity.

And when the going gets tough:

- Hold people to account, but never be derogatory, demeaning or attacking.

  Top tip: focus on problem-solving.

2 Remove barriers to high performance

You are two months into your role, and it is a timely opportunity to sense-check what might be holding the team back from greater levels of performance.

Spot check for the possible barriers to team high performance:

- Weak leadership
- Wrong mission
- Wrong people
- Unclear roles and responsibilities
- Inadequate systems and technology
- Lack of trust
- Fear of conflict
- Lack of commitment
- Silo-thinking
- No accountability
- Group think

WEAK LEADERSHIP

- *Are you leading the team effectively?*

some leaders never actually step up and take charge of the team

Some leaders never actually step up and take charge of the team. In other words, they are weak leaders. You may have this book, and know all the theory of leading a team in your first 100 days, but may also not be assertive enough to really take charge of your team in practice. It is almost a taboo thing to say, but some leaders are afraid of their teams and let their teams take charge of them. I mentioned that I have seen this happen where the leader is held hostage to some strong personalities on the team. For example, when the HR person on the team starts telling the leader what he or she can or can't do, regardless of the business rationale, doesn't that mean that the HR person is in charge rather than the business person? The same could be said when the Finance Director takes too much control. Don't be one of those weak leaders, trying to please other people, trying too hard to keep the team happy and being overly cautious about bureaucracy and rules. You are the boss. You are supposed to be the one in charge. Assert yourself.

WRONG MISSION

● *Did you set out the wrong team mission?*
I am not suggesting that you aim to do a u-turn on your team mission so soon, but after two months you need to check on whether all is what it seemed and that your course of action is the correct one. If you start to realise that your team mission or team direction is wrong or needs to be adjusted then it is better to have the courage to change course now, rather than to wait any longer. At least you will have reset the team mission before the end of your first 100 days.

WRONG PEOPLE

● *Are the right people in place?*
Armed now with 60 days of experience of working

with members of this team, you are in a good position to review the quality of people you have on board. How would you rate your satisfaction levels with the people on your team – high, medium or low? This is not about whether you like people, but about whether

if you have known incompetents and underperformers on the team, then now is the time to face it

you are confident that you have the right people on board and that they are motivated, competent and delivering results. If you have known incompetents and underperformers on the team, then now is the time to face it. Either put them on a process for training and development and assess again at a later stage – or think about moving them off your team. Doing nothing with underperformers is not an option. Well, it is an option, but one that you will live to regret because ignoring the problem won't solve it.

Spotting and dealing with underperformers

At 60 days, you should have enough information and experience to spot an underperforming team member. To help you arrive at a conclusion on whether you have one or more underperformers on your team, take a step back and run each member through the 'skill, will, fit' test:

- Skill – has this person demonstrated sufficient skill and ability to do their job and deliver results?
- Will – has this person demonstrated the right attitude and willingness to step up their game?
- Fit – does this person fit the high standards you expect from members of your team?

Underperformers do not serve you or their team mates. As soon as possible, begin the HR process of removing underperformers from your team. This is a moment in the executive's life when they may choose denial and avoidance rather than deal with the problem – or, worse, decide that as 'heroic' leader they will be the one to inspire the underperformers towards greatness. My advice is plain and simple. Demote or divest yourself of your underperformers in your first 100 days. It is the right thing to do, and it will also be much harder to do it later when you may have less freedom to make fast personnel decisions.

UNCLEAR ROLES AND RESPONSIBILITIES

● *Are roles and responsibilities clear?*

Do people know what their job is? Sounds obvious enough, but some people may be defining their role as something other than what you expect or need from them. Although this may seem odd, I suggest that you take some time out to ask people individually what they believe their role is. It is always interesting to hear the other person's perspective on how they see their own role. Be aware that with some team members, a form of passive aggression exists when someone on the team does not agree with or does not like what you have asked them to do, but doesn't voice their opinion and keeps doing the role the way they want to do it. Check if this is happening with anyone on your team and, if it is, you need to address it.

INADEQUATE SYSTEMS AND TECHNOLOGY

● *Are the right systems in place?*

Check whether the necessary IT, MIS and other

knowledge systems are in place and functioning effectively to support the activity of your team. You don't want to be ignorant of a situation whereby your performance is being stymied by people not having access to information on which to base their decisions.

LACK OF TRUST

● *Does trust exist?*

The biggest obstacle to team performance is absence of trust. When trust breaks down, then everybody second guesses the motives of everybody else, decisions take longer and some decisions never get made. Whereas when trust exists, there are lots of givens and no need for multiple checks and the team achieves a great performance flow. Politics amongst team members is very draining for everyone involved and, at two **be alert to any cliques forming within the team** months in, you need to be alert to any cliques forming within the team. Naturally there will be friendship groups within the team, but check whether it has gone beyond natural groupings and tipped into unhelpful clique behaviour.

FEAR OF CONFLICT

● *Is there a fear of conflict?*

Are team members afraid to speak their mind? If yes, then you have an issue on your hands. Without healthy debates, and differences of opinion, how can you truly sense-check any of the results coming out of the team? Absence of conflict is as unhealthy as too much conflict.

As leader of the team, you need to encourage people to express their opinions. If necessary, set up role plays where people are given overt permission to take the opposite stance of a proposed decision under debate. When team members can openly challenge each other, and debate pros and cons, then you will have a livelier working dynamic and people will be forced to work harder to defend their positions. Like any iterative process, this is what can take a draft one proposal to a much more robust draft two proposal, with new ideas or better solutions included.

LACK OF COMMITMENT

● *How committed are your team members?*

In the context of seeking to achieve high performance, you need to have committed team members on board – not people who turn up to simply put the hours in. Is there a sense of can-do and optimism on the team? Complainers are very energy-draining. Give me 'will' over 'skill' any day, in the sense that someone who really wants to do a good job can be trained and will appreciate the investment, whereas a very skilled person who is apathetic is of very little value-add to the team.

SILO-THINKING

● *Is there too much silo-thinking?*

When team members are overly concerned with leading their individual silo functions, then true teaming is not taking place. Team members need to be able to set aside their silo-thinking, and come to team meetings as contributors not takers. When team members turn up for a team meeting, are they still wearing their silo hat, or can they bring their best leadership selves to the table and make compromises for the greater good?

NO ACCOUNTABILITY

● *Are your people held to account for lack of results?*

It can happen that you have total clarity on direction, a great roadmap, but no one is being held to account for delivering their actions or their section of the plan. The worst feeling for a leader at the @60days milestone is to realise that team members are all talk and no action.

At the milestone review workshops, and at key interim status meetings, check that your team members are delivering what they said they would deliver. Instil a discipline of what I call 'on time, on budget' and don't be lenient when you see

instil a discipline of 'on time, on budget' and don't be lenient when you see deviations from the plan

deviations from the plan. Sometimes the leader is so busy building consensus that he is not holding people strictly to account. Be assertive on standards for accountability.

GROUP THINK

● *Is the group overly cohesive, to the detriment of better outcomes?*

Group think refers to situations in which the members of the group focus more on conforming their views to what they believe is the consensus view than on exploring alternatives. It tends to occur in highly cohesive groups that have an illusion of invulnerability and whose members are not critical of one another's ideas. The results can be dumbed down, bad or irrational decisions.

3 Communication, communication, communication

The importance of getting communication right from the start cannot be overstated. At the beginning of leading the team in your first 100 days, there is a lot of communication going on. You are eager to meet people, and they are eager to meet you. Two months later, there is a danger that the intensity of the communication has waned. So it is time to reinforce the importance of what it takes to be a good communicator, and to remind you that you need to ensure that communication levels are in a good place.

two months later, there is a danger that the intensity of the communication has waned

- Be clear
- Be timely
- Be engaging
- Be empathetic
- Be transparent
- Be action-oriented
- Be emotionally aware

BE CLEAR

There is nothing worse for a team member than hearing an instruction from their boss that they simply don't understand.

They may try to repeatedly check what you are saying, or they may go back to their desk and wait until they feel more confident to check what you mean. Sometimes they may never check, and a month later you wonder why your instructions were not carried out. You need to be as clear as possible each time you ask for something to be done: say what you want done, by when. You don't need to always explain how, as hopefully your team members are responsible and capable enough to perform the how.

You can wait for the deliverable date to check for understanding, but this is the slow approach. You may discover that the deliverable is not what you wanted or expected, and now further time needs to elapse while you attempt to get clearer with your communication. The better and faster way to figure out whether a team member understands your instruction is for you to be as clear as possible about what you want, and then check for understanding from the other person. Don't say 'do you understand?' as the only answer to that question from a team member not wanting to lose face in front of his boss, is surely 'yes' regardless of actual understanding. Instead, find ways to ask the person to play back to you what they heard. For example, you could do this verbally in conversation, or you could ask for a short brief or update document by the end of the week – describing the current situation, key issues and next steps. You will only learn whether you are a clear communicator when the instruction matches what you said, and includes the deliverable date.

BE TIMELY

It is not just about what you communicate, but also when you communicate. Timing is important to foster good communication amongst the team. If you delay your requests, or ask for extra deliverables when the deadline is already stretched, then team members are going to become frustrated with you.

If you have bad news to share with some team members, such as upcoming redundancies, then be sensitive to the timing of the news. For example, it may be more appropriate to give people redundancy news on a Friday so that they have time and space to process it over the weekend, without being expected to just behave like business as usual the very next day.

BE ENGAGING

When you communicate with other people, you have the opportunity to engage them. Depending on your tone, or manner, or mood you may lose this opportunity and inadvertently de-motivate team members by sounding bad-tempered or impatient. Communication is about relating your views and wishes and responses to other humans, usually to evoke a positive response – so be mindful of what you see, how you sound when you say it, and what effect you are having on the other person.

BE EMPATHETIC

Communication works best when it is a two-way dynamic. The great thing about communication is that we can fix it as we go, by trying new approaches depending on the responses we receive. For example, if the other person sounds tired, you can empathise and take a moment to enquire about how they are feeling – and then move on to the task.

BE TRANSPARENT

Transparency is the watchword of the moment because of the fallout from poor corporate behaviours that led to the global economic meltdown. Whatever the reasons, transparency and sharing as new phenomena are here to stay and as a leader you need to be willing to share more about your plans than traditionally. People want to know what is going on, and are less willing to take instruction unless they know why you are issuing the instruction.

transparency is the watchword of the moment

BE ACTION-ORIENTED

Communicate with energy, and inspire people towards action. Use your communication moments as opportunities to kick start renewed action towards achievement of goals. Don't stop at the message; translate the message into next steps and what actions need to take place from here. Communicate the message, and communicate the action required to tangibilise the message.

BE EMOTIONALLY AWARE

Leaders typically don't like to think about feelings, but you need to realise that emotions play a large role in the success or failure of the team. When the team is angry, it is unlikely to be high performing. The team may decide to down tools and refuse to do any work at all. You don't always have to have a happy team, because as discussed earlier it is healthy for conflict to exist within a team. However, as leader of the team, the ability to sense the mood in the room and have a feel for the mood of the team means that you are better equipped on how to communicate to

don't ignore the emotional life of the group

the team. Get to know your team's default moods so that you can sense when there are any deviations from the norm. For example, if the team seems unusually quiet, take this as a cue to ask if anything is wrong. If the team seem unusually buoyant, find out why. Don't ignore the emotional life of the group. Be alert to gathering the clues on the moods and feelings of the team and you will become a better communicator.

4 Update your First 100 Days Team Plan

As a final part of your @60 Days Team Workshop, the team need to refresh and reset the next 30 days' actions.

The rigour and discipline of updating your First 100 Days Team Plan at monthly milestones will reap significant benefits for you:

- The team stays focused on what really matters.
- Each element of the seven-part formula for team success is thoroughly considered and kept top of mind.
- The team is motivated by coming together and tracking its own performance.
- Team members share the experience of solving problems together.
- Any early issues are ironed out and resolved, in an appropriate forum.
- A clear direction is reset for the next 30 days.

You should recognise that this is a key moment of importance. You and your team are now over half way through your first 100 days team journey. You are about to enter into your team's final 30-day window of activity within the plan. As leader, you need to feel assured that you and your team are more than half way through your plan in terms of what it will take to achieve your desired outcomes by the end of your first 100 days.

Update First 100 Days Team Plan

AT THE END OF YOUR @60 DAYS TEAM WORKSHOP

Refresh and reset the actions for the next 30 days, based on your first 60 days' experience, and on:

- a review of progress against the First 100 Days Team Plan;
- performance accelerator tactics to remove barriers to high performance;
- performance accelerator tactics to improve communication.

First100™ Caselet 3

THE LEADER WHO TRIED TO CONTROL TOO MUCH

Kamran decided that the only way he could lead his company effectively as CEO would be if he knew everything that was going on. Rather than rely on a hierarchy of direct reports, he decided that he would create a very flat teaming structure. He established a Top 15 and a Top 35 amongst his organisation and he set up a regular system of meetings whereby every person within those groups reported directly into him. This made him feel more secure – and he felt that the calibre of the team versus the pressure of the delivery requirements of the team meant that he simply had no choice but to organise his people in this way.

One hundred days later and Kamran was controlling everything and everyone. Team members belonging

▶

to Kamran's key groups were unable to make a decision without first getting Kamran's approval. Kamran was exhausted from constant monitoring of everybody's work, and started to wonder why his team members were not taking initiative or getting faster results. With a total lack of awareness about the effect that he himself had caused, Kamran got more and more frustrated with team members. The team was afraid of Kamran, and his temper. When Kamran was in a good mood, the whole company was in a good mood. When Kamran was in a bad mood, everyone took shelter as far away from him as possible. Results were good, but were driven in a climate of fear. Results were attributed to Kamran, but in fact the results were driven by the firm's product set and operating model. The core activities of the firm meant that the business operated like an automatic cash machine, much like how a bank is set up simply to receive money, regardless of the quality of the leadership in place.

Kamran did not plan on disempowering his team. He simply did not know how to be a leader. Eventually the situation imploded a year later, when the Board conducted a values survey across the organisation. Less than 5 per cent of Kamran's team cited him as a role model and less than 3 per cent felt he lived up to the corporate values. The Board found Kamran to be a charismatic and dynamic individual, but upon deeper investigation it became clear that Kamran's behaviour did not meet the acceptable leadership standard for the organisation. Kamran was totally blind-sided on the day he was asked to leave the company.

The moral of the story

Leadership as control freak is not a sustainable approach. Learn how to empower your followers, and realise that you will feel more in control when you trust your team. Some organisations make money, regardless of the quality of leadership – and this gets confused with those in charge assuming that it is their skills that have led to great results. In the past, has the business model masked your flaws as a leader, and is now the time and opportunity to switch from control mindset to empowerment mindset?

5 Advice from the executive front line

By day 60 you should be in a situation where you've assessed your direct reports and you're starting to build the top-team.

Keith Wilson, Global HR Director, Astrazeneca

Beyond core objectives, a new to role leader needs to be capable of exerting influence, often in a subtle and indirect manner.

Elaine Maclean, Group HR Director, Legal & General

Get in the habit of having one-to-ones with your direct reports early and often. Have a high frequency of team meetings, but remember, these don't have to be long [in duration].

John Harker, Group HR Director, Al-Futtaim

A leader joining from outside the business needs to stamp their authority without alienating the team ... there are great benefits to doing things on a collegiate basis.

Andrew Golding, CEO, Kent Reliance

*By now [after 60 days] you should have buy-in from your
key stakeholders. Otherwise you truly are in a crisis
situation.*

**John Coburn, Head of EMEA Learning and
Development, McAfee**

*Active listening is the most important activity a new leader can
undertake. As well as building an understanding of your people,
you need to show what your values are, what you stand for and
who you are as a leader.*

**Phil Bishop, HR Chief Operating Officer, Lloyds
Banking Group**

*Bringing clarity around the team's purpose and how this
fits with the business strategy is vital. The leader needs to
acknowledge the importance of the team itself and instil belief
around what can be achieved.*

John Handley, HR Director, International Markets, Bupa

*After 60 days in role you need to be bringing a real sense of
purpose to what you are doing, and keep your energy levels
high. Taking the time to reflect on achievements to date will
energise you, and will also show you whether you need to
modify your approach or direction.*

**Mark Waight, Director of Group Management
Development, Logica**

*After a couple of months in role, your message should be refined
so that it is tangible, understandable and real.*

Richard Gartside, HR Director, Balfour Beatty

*Ensure there is buy-in from direct reports, and that they feel
you have taken on board their views. Even more important is
showing that you are a delivery-focused leader. As far as you
can, communicate frequently with your team around what is*

happening, and why. Rumours will be created to fill any gaps you leave.

Ian Hood, Group e-Business Director, RSA Insurance

Outline your vision and continually check performance and team decisions against that vision.

Paul Breslin, General Manager EMEA, PopCap

part three

End

6

@90 days: Sprint to the end

- Review progress against team plan
- Write your team's final 10-day 'to-do' list
- Gather feedback and air any issues
- Take time out for team reflection
- Advice from the executive front line

1 Review progress against team plan

You can keep the team plan on track by conducting thorough progress reviews of the First 100 Days Team Plan with your team at the key milestones of @30 days, @60 days and @90 days.

The @90 days milestone is the final major pause and opportunity to review team progress against your First 100 Days Team Plan.

Don't underestimate the opportunity to also use the @90 Days Team Workshop to facilitate the acceleration of the all-important working and social bond between leader and team, and amongst the team itself.

Review progress against First 100 Days Team Plan
@90 DAYS TEAM WORKSHOP

1 Review your First 100 Days Team Plan.

2 Are you and your team on track to achieve the 90-day milestones set out in the plan?

3 Are you and your team where you expected to be @90 days?

4 Take stock of what is working well/not well with your Team Plan @90 days:
   - What more can you and the team do to improve performance against plan?
   - Brainstorm solutions to any blocks/challenges.
   - Think about the performance acceleration opportunities.
   - Who can help you and the team with this exercise, and act as your sounding board/advisor?

At this point, you only have 10 days left. Make the most of them by having a very energising @90 Days Team Workshop. The @90 Days Team Workshop is a good opportunity to review progress, facilitate team bonding and to encourage the development of positive cultural norms within the team – whilst ensuring total focus on achieving the end of 100 days deadline for delivery on the team plan.

Top tips for @90 Days Team Workshop:

- Be very focused on the 100-day deadline.

    Top tip: schedule a meeting with your boss or other important team stakeholder for the approximate time of the 100-day deadline, where your team will present their First 100 Days' achievements. This will focus the team's mind on making sure they hit the deadline.

- Use the meeting to agree the final 10-day 'to-do' list.

    Top tip: raise the energy levels on the team by bringing in outside stimulus such as a pep talk from your boss, or having the meeting at an interesting new location.

- Use the meeting to give and receive feedback.

    Top tip: bring in an external consultant to run an effective two-way leader–team feedback giving and receiving session, and facilitate a 'look back' session on lessons learned.

- Use the meeting to surface any major conflict or teaming issues.

    Top tip: if serious conflicts within the team are going to be aired, you may want to bring in the specialist support of a team mediator.

- Raise the bar, again, on standards and behaviours amongst team members.

    Top tip: use the feedback giving and receiving as a fresh opportunity to reset the bar on team standards and behaviours.

- Check throughout the meeting for inhibitions to free expression, including:
  - people not wanting to appear to be the only objector;
  - concerns that if they dissent then they will not be considered to be a team player.

  Top tip: from time to time, remind people that you welcome objections/debate/alternative views.

- Check for group think, i.e. too much group cohesion, and too quick to rush to one answer.

  Top tip: openly raise the issue of group think, and put someone in charge of spotting group think.

And, when the going gets tough:

- Hold people to account, but never be derogatory, demeaning or attacking.

  Top tip: focus on problem-solving.

2 Write your team's final 10-day 'to-do' list

take the final 10 days as an opportunity to make an energetic sprint to the end

Ideally, you want to complete your whole First 100 Days Team Plan but, with only 10 days left, it may be a matter of prioritisation on what can realistically be achieved by the team by the end of the first 100 days. Get practical on what can be completed on the team plan and take the final 10 days as an opportunity to make an energetic sprint to the end.

WHAT ARE THE URGENT AND IMPORTANT PRIORITIES FOR THE NEXT 10 DAYS?

It may feel obvious, at first, such as the completion of one key deliverable. However, rather than a narrow view, allow some time in your @90 Days Team Workshop to run through each of the seven parts of the leader–team success formula to think about final 10-day actions to be completed on each of them to achieve the individual sub-outcome and to achieve the overall desired outcome within the next 10 days.

- Role model
- Mission setter
- Recruiter
- Communicator
- Motivator
- Skills builder
- Target maker

With your team, agree the final 10-day to-do list. Agree what to complete as per the team plan, plus:

ON ROLE MODEL

> What symbolic act can you do today or in the next 10 days to demonstrate you are a leadership role model? For example, where there are key pressure points within the team you could offer extra time or resources, or get directly involved yourself on working through the issues. Is there a difficult stakeholder to deal with, or a difficult decision to be taken? Show your team that you care about the pressure that they are under, and

demonstrate that you are prepared to go the extra mile to support them.

ON MISSION SETTER

Ask each member on the team to play back to you what the team mission is – check for any misalignments.

ON RECRUITER

If not already decided, make final decisions on who stays and who goes from the team.

ON COMMUNICATOR

Communicate to your team that you are in the final 10 days and that the emphasis is now on being completer–finishers and hitting the end of first 100 days deadline.

ON MOTIVATOR

Think about what you can do to improve motivation levels on the team in the final 10 days. For example, agree that there will be a team celebration event at end of 100 days.

ON SKILLS BUILDER

Pay attention as to whether you have a team of completer–finishers ready and able to drive towards a final deadline or whether this is a skill gap that needs to be addressed now and going forward.

ON TARGET MAKER

Check in again with constituent team stakeholders on who expects what to be delivered, by when. If it is clear that your team is not going to hit the timelines for expected delivery, then the next 10 days as target-maker may require you and your team to reset and manage expectations of stakeholders.

3 Gather feedback and air any issues

The @90days milestone review workshop is a great opportunity to give and receive feedback in a formal and structured way. You guys have worked as a team for three months and it is a good time to take stock and check in with each other on how the team is functioning and whether it is living up to your standards for a high-performing team.

There are four aspects to consider:

- leader to team feedback;
- leader to individual team member feedback;
- stakeholder feedback to the team;
- team to leader feedback.

LEADER TO TEAM FEEDBACK

This section provides you with ideas on how to feedback to your team as a whole group.

'surprises good, surprises bad'

Tell your team what surprised you over the past 90 days, and divide it into those things that were unexpected positives and those that were unexpected negatives. This is a lively and interesting way of relaying your experience versus your expectations.

On surprises-good, use praise as a way of reinforcing good behaviour and reminding people of your standards for this team, and their standards for each other:

For example:

> I expected you guys to be committed, and enthusiastic, but I was positively surprised by the lengths that you would go to hit key deadlines. For example when that proposal had to go out on Monday, I was impressed by how everyone pulled together as a team, and some even worked over the weekend to ensure that we got it in on time. It impresses me that when the pressure is on, the team will go the extra mile to deliver.

On surprises-bad, use standard-setting as a way of reinforcing that you have high standards and the team needs to continuously strive to achieve those standards. Use the opportunity of a negative surprise to reset the bar on high standards for the team.

For example:

> I expected you guys to be committed, and enthusiastic, so I was surprised in a bad way that when it really mattered, you guys don't raise your game to hit key deadlines. For example, when that proposal had to go out on Monday, you guys missed the deadline. It felt like perhaps you were all talk and no action. I was not impressed by the lack of teaming, and lack of effort. On this team, I expect us to deliver on time, on budget. No exceptions. We need to remind ourselves of our standards and our desire to be a high-performing team, and realise that if

we miss major deadlines then we are not going to be taken seriously by others in the organisation.

no feedback-sandwiches

Don't do what is called a 'feedback-sandwich', which is to say something positive, then say something negative, and then say something positive to quickly cover up any feelings of discomfort. Instead, when you communicate the surprises-bad, allow the negatives/'opportunities to do better' to sink in; allow time for the team to feel uncomfortable about not adhering to your high standards. Then focus on how to resolve the negatives, and on what the team can do to strive to reach the higher standard expected.

LEADER TO INDIVIDUAL TEAM MEMBER FEEDBACK

You also need to give members of the team your individual feedback.

As part of your preparation for your first 100 days of leading this team, you took a views on the team you were inheriting, based on the data available and the perceptions of others. Now that you are 90 days in, it is a great opportunity to make a more informed, fresh realisations on what you have, based on your first-hand experience.

Having worked with team members for three months, having synthesised your own views, having heard the view of stakeholders, you will have the experience of who has stepped up or not, and who has delivered against the team plan.

- Who has delivered?
- Who has stepped up?
- Is my successor on this team?
- Who has the drive to go further?
- Who has the potential to go further?

- Who is a good leader of his/her own team?
- How did each person respond to the feedback?
- Who gave me useful feedback, who had good insights?
- What did the stakeholder feedback tell me about team members?
- Who stays and who goes?

Set up one-to-ones to give individual team members feedback and take the opportunity to reset the leadership standard required.

Consider using the following set of criteria for the discussions, and rank people on where you think they are versus where they need to be on each one:

REQUIRED INTELLIGENCES FOR MY TEAM MEMBERS	RANKING: HIGH	RANKING: MEDIUM	RANKING: LOW
SQ – strategic intelligence You understand the bigger picture, and contribute to the team strategy and plans.			
IQ – intellectual/knowledge/technical intelligence You have the knowledge and competence required to deliver your role. You share your knowledge with others to support their learning and delivery.			
EQ – emotional intelligence You demonstrate a positive mental mindset. You regulate your emotions and support a positive team atmosphere.			
BQ – behavioural intelligence You behave appropriately with others, conduct yourself well at meetings and impress customers and key stakeholders.			

TQ – teaming intelligence You are a high-functioning, high-contributing member of the team. You can rise above your individual agenda to pursue the team's shared agenda.			
RQ – results intelligence You demonstrate a delivery mindset, and you know how to drive projects to completion. You take accountability for completion of tasks. You know how to get things done in this team and this organisation.			

You should give one-to-one feedback to each team member:

- Ask the person to rank himself.

- Share your view on that person's team intelligences rankings.

- Summarise your feedback by way of *'Do more of/do less of'.*

- You could also share your views on strengths/ development areas within:
    - their job (what their function is);
    - their role (how they contribute to the team, e.g. 'the enthusiast', 'the creative');
    - their value-add (key strength);
    - developmental opportunity (key block/area for improvement).

By now, as part of the recruiter role that you have been playing as leader of the team, you should have already figured out who is staying and who is going, but if for any reason there is a lingering question mark over anyone – or the feedback has surfaced an issue with someone that means you no longer want them as part of your team – then act now. The last 90 days should have

decide who you want to keep on your team

given you enough experience and insight to decide who you want to keep on your team.

As a useful exercise, you could also put together a 'team matrix', with each team member, on a one-pager to see what you've got, and how people compare against one another, and as a sense-check of what gaps there may be, for individuals and for the team as a whole.

	JOHN	GARRETT	FIONA	AOIBHE	SHAY	MUIREANN	SARAH	DAVID	SOPHIE
SQ	X							X	
IQ	X	X	X	X	X	X	X	X	X
EQ				X			X		X
BQ	X			X				X	X
TQ	X	X	X		X	X	X		X
RQ		X	X	X	X	X	X	X	

STAKEHOLDER FEEDBACK TO THE TEAM

At the @90 days mark, choose approximately three to five stakeholders to ask for feedback on the team's performance and ability to meet stakeholder expectations and requirements. These stakeholders should be key 'customers' of the team, and rely on the team for key deliverables or services.

You can gather the feedback directly, or ask a facilitator to conduct the exercise. Depending on the situation, perhaps it is better if this time you gather the feedback instead of a facilitator. I say this because it can be an opportunity for you at the @90 days mark to reach out to team stakeholders and build a relationship with them. Stakeholders will appreciate that you are doing it in the context of wanting to serve them better, and that symbolic gesture alone will serve you well.

It is reasonable to ask stakeholders to be available for 20–30 minutes to give feedback. Phone calls work great for stakeholder feedback-gathering because 'with initial prompting' they then start sharing stream-of-consciousness views down the telephone line.

Stakeholder rating of the team should consider the following:

- *Alignment of expectations*: does the team consistently meet or exceed your expectations?
- *Quality of delivery*: are the team deliverables at, below or above the quality levels you require?
- *Timeliness*: does the team ever miss deadlines or does it always deliver on time?
- *Value-add*: how does the team add value to you, your business, your needs?
- *Advice*: do you have any advice for the team, and the leader, on areas for improvement?

When you have gathered the feedback, synthesise it into key themes/key learnings to be shared and discussed with your team.

TEAM TO LEADER FEEDBACK

After 90 days of working together, this is a timely opportunity to get formal feedback on your leadership approach from your team.

Ask an external consultant or HR person to facilitate the session on team to leader feedback. This signals that you are serious about the exercise. Set the tone for the session by introducing the facilitator and expressing your desire for open and honest commentary – then you can leave the room, further indicating that this is a sincere exercise and that you want to provide a safe environment for the team to provide fair and frank feedback. Your team will feel better about discussing your strengths and development opportunities if you are not in the room. A skilled facilitator should be able to spot feedback themes, patterns, and draw out insights from the spoken and unspoken cues of the team members.

Brief the facilitator

Let the facilitator know that what you want from the session is:

- open, honest commentary in a safe environment;
- fair and frank feedback on how you can improve your leadership skills;
- summary rankings as high, medium or low on the following topics, ideally with examples:
  - general leadership impact to date;
  - on strategy; ability to set a clear direction;
  - on people; ability to bring people with you;
  - on leadership values; sets high standards and is a good role model;
  - strengths; unique spikes and contributions;
  - weaknesses; areas for further development;
  - advice to the leader; top tips;
- feedback of the headline results/themes to you without attributing who said what.

I cannot overstate the hugely positive impact of such an exercise on the team and their perception of you. Even before you run the session, just by stating that you plan to run a facilitated feedback session, you will get an upsurge of respect and admiration. As the leader of the team, to lay yourself open to feedback in this way is very impressive and your team knows it takes guts, and will admire you for it.

I appreciate that it can be tough for any leader to open up to being vulnerable in this way, but remember, it is a sign of strength and confidence to be open to feedback. If the facilitator is professional, then the session will be a win-win for everyone involved – your team get to let off some steam if they are having challenges with you, and you get to address any brewing problems early on.

Be ready to handle receiving tough feedback

- Always treat the feedback as a gift. It offers you insight on how your team perceive you. It gives you the opportunity **always treat the feedback as a gift** to understand what matters to them. You can potentially clear up any misunderstandings, plus you can use the information to further hone your leadership skills.

- Whether or not you like what you hear, always say thank you.

- Don't be defensive, don't say anything at first. Just listen.

- Check for understanding. Say things like 'Thank you, can you tell me more about that?'

- Don't try to work out who said what.

- Be ready to structure your response as follows:
  - what I can respond to today
  - what I can respond to at a later date.

  This buys you some time, if you don't have a response to some issues raised.

- Choose at least one thing that you agree to take immediate action on, as this demonstrates to the team that you plan on taking action on the feedback received.

How you respond to the feedback is a real test of your character as a leader, and your team know it. They will be avidly observing how well or not well you can take tough messages. If you are defensive, or even get angry, then they will take this as their cue to no longer be honest with you. After all, what would be the point, if you don't listen?

So, please realise that this is an important moment in your relationship with your team. Be ready to receive tough messages, and be ready to handle them maturely.

Know what to do if feedback is all good
If for any reason, the feedback is very light, such as no issues and keep doing what you are doing, then sack the facilitator and re-do the exercise. Encourage the team to be more honest and opinionated during the next feedback giving session. After all, if you don't learn anything from the exercise, then it is a waste of everybody's time.

Be honest with yourself. Was the feedback very light because your team members are afraid of you? Is trust so low on the team, that the 'safe environment' didn't feel safe enough? Or perhaps your team members are a bit weak, or don't really care, and don't want to do anything to rock the boat – if so, you need to toughen them up and let them know that they should expect high standards from themselves and their leader.

There is no such thing as no room for improvement when it comes to leadership skills and standards.

4 Take time out for team reflection

Following all of the feedback gathering and giving/receiving, you need to organise a follow-up 'team retreat' session for you guys to detach yourselves from the day to day, and honestly face up to what is working well and not well with the team. Taking time out to reflect on performance can be a massive performance accelerator. Issues can be unblocked, misunderstandings can be resolved, barriers come down and bonds strengthen.

taking time out to reflect on performance can be a massive performance accelerator

If there are serious conflict issues that emerged from the feedback that need to be aired and resolved, you may want to hire in the professional services of a consultant or facilitator who can surface and address issues in a managed way.

Getting everyone out of the office to work in very pleasant surroundings such as a conference centre or hotel can be incredibly effective as a method of getting people out of the detail and focusing more on the bigger picture. Taking a full day out off-site sets the scene for the team to be more reflective and more strategic. I urge you to stay focused on the task which is about reflection and improvement of team performance. Don't let your team get distracted by the excitement of getting out of the office. I am not a big fan of typical 'team away days' involving corporate team-building activities such as using maps to find treasure in the hills, and building rafts to journey to the other side of the river – and so forth. I question the value and productiveness of such events. For your first off-site event, keep the team retreat focused on the task at hand.

TAKE TIME OUT TO REFLECT ON THE FEEDBACK

Consider:

- What has the feedback taught us?
- What do we need to start doing, stop doing and continue doing?

- How did we handle the feedback? Are we open enough as a team?
- How do we turn the feedback into a clear action plan and next steps?

TAKE TIME OUT TO REFLECT ON HOW YOU RANK YOURSELVES AS A HIGH-PERFORMING TEAM

Are we creating the right conditions for our success as a high-performing team?

- How do we respond to feedback?
- How do we respond to pressure and change?
- Are we passionate and stimulated by our work? Are we using all our talents?
- Are we fostering an environment to support new ideas and breakthroughs?
- Do we have the right working practices and management approaches in place?
- Do we function on trust? Are we adhering to high-value standards and living our values?
- Are we effective across borders and engaging with other teams, or are we too closed off?
- Do team members feel accountable, empowered and believe they are reaching their potential?
- Do team members like being part of this team? Are there sufficient opportunities on offer?

Reflect on the feedback; surface the issues, resolve conflicts, convert lessons learned into an action plan with clear next steps and accountabilities and review mechanism, and then move on.

TEAM FEEDBACK	ACTION PLAN	ACTION OWNER	FIRST STEPS	REVIEW DATE
Lessons learned				

TAKE TIME OUT TO REFLECT ON WHETHER YOU ARE AN EFFECTIVE LEADER OF THIS TEAM

As well as the team reflecting on its progress, you now also need to take some time out on your own – or with the help of a consultant – to go through your own personal reflection on how well you are leading this team.

- Think about what worked well, what didn't, what needs to happen next.
- Write down your lessons learned, internalise them and move on.

Key leadership watch-outs @90 days:

- *Are you addressing conflict in the team?*

don't 'outsource' problem team members to HR or anyone else

If the evidence shows that there are issues, don't try to pretend a people problem does not exist, or that conflict does not exist. Don't 'outsource' problem team members to HR or anyone else. Front up to any people issues yourself.

- *Are you asserting yourself as leader of the team?*

  Being assertive is very aligned to your self-confidence as a leader. It is not about pleasing people (weak self-confidence), and it is not about being 'overly' assertive either (another form of weak self-confidence that can tip into unhealthy aggression). Being assertive is about being very calm, and grounded, knowing what you want from your team and continuously communicating what you want until you get it.

- *Are you too quick to seek reassurance from team members?*

  It can happen that newly appointed leaders are overly

keen on seeking out the reassurance of members of their management team, and being overly malleable to their influences, when making a decision or planning the way forward. Seek opinions yes, seek input yes, but then make up your own mind on what to do. Looking for reassurance is a sign of lack of confidence in your own leadership abilities. Seeking reassurance is like asking for 'permission' from others. You don't need permission from members of your team. You are the person in charge. Learn to self-validate.

- *Are you too keen on building consensus?*

  The modern approach on leading teams is to go for less command-and-control and focus more on building consensus amongst team members. Consensus-building makes sense a lot of the time; because when you have the buy-in of the team, it follows that the team are more likely to be agreeable and productive. However, please remember that the consensus-building approach is just one method for achieving your desired outcomes, and it is not the only one – other methods can be deployed too, depending on the situation. Consensus-building goes wrong as a method of achieving outcomes when the leader prioritises consensus-building over what are the best outcomes for the business. The leader can seek out opinions but has to have the courage to make unpopular decisions as and when it is necessary for the greater good of the business.

5 Advice from the executive front line

At this point [100 days in] you should have stamped your authority without alienating your team. If you have achieved this then you have made a successful transition.

Tony Williams, Director of Human Resources, RBS Global Banking & Markets

By the end of 100 days your capacity to do the job will be clear to you and to everyone else.

Marcus Millership, Head of Human Resources, Shared Services, Rolls Royce

Trust your direct reports until they give you a reason not to. Engage with teams below your direct reports to get a fuller picture of the challenge facing you and your team. Treat your direct reports and other stakeholders as adults, and be open and transparent.

Lisa Anson, Marketing Company President, Astrazeneca

You need to listen to everyone and then make your own mind up.

Jojar Dhinsa, Chairman, The Athlone Group

100 days will have given you enough time to establish yourself, but you will still have fresh eyes, allowing you to see where there is scope for improvement.

Shiree Murdoch, Director of HR & Development, Nabarro

You need to look at the first 100 days as the time when you make your mark and set yourself up for longer-term success.

Faran Johnson, Group HR Director, Clear Channel International

In the first 100 days you must demonstrate a real interest in your people and their lives both inside and outside of work, without being intrusive. As you get to know your team, recognise the diversity each person brings and remember that you don't need to have a natural affinity with all of them as people to have a good working relationship and a great team.

Nikki Walker, Senior Director, Inclusion & Diversity Europe, Cisco

The first 100 days is a rich source of learning for a new leader but also a key period to make an impact on your main stakeholders. Friction is inevitable, but you can show what type of leader you are in how you deal with it.

David Hindley, Human Resources Director (R&D), Danone

Finish your First 100 Days

- Close out your First 100 Days Team Plan
- Record team achievements and capture lessons learned
- Communicate team success to stakeholders
- Celebrate with your team
- Reset team objectives and renew the endeavour

1 Close out your First 100 Days Team Plan

There is a point when the first 100 days journey for the team is over, and that point has now been reached. With a timeline process such as 100 days, there is a natural timeline ending. Yet some leaders find it difficult to close out the First 100 Days process and draw a line under it.

Perhaps it is because an ending forces you to review the journey and acknowledge that maybe you and your team did not achieve everything that you set out to achieve. Perhaps it is because you and your team are so busy, day to day, that you don't want to set aside the time to acknowledge that the process is over. Perhaps it is because you and your team have been running so fast that you prefer to keep striving and achieving, rather than acknowledge that it is time to stop, wrap up the first 100 days process, draw a line under it and reset the goals and possibilities for the next phase.

wrap up the first 100 days process, draw a line under it and reset the goals and possibilities

The benefits of effectively closing out the First 100 Days Team Plan are as follows:

- *Being able to recognise when to say 'we're done':*
  As a leader, you need to learn how to create a positive ending with your team, whether for the first 100 days process or for other critical projects. There is nothing more frustrating for team stakeholders if projects just drift on, rather than come to a neat and satisfactory conclusion. Some teams get so excited by beginnings

that they become addicted to starting new projects, without satisfactorily closing out any existing ones. In time, this becomes an excessive drain on team resources as multiple projects are underway, and none are being closed off.

● *Being able to review the journey:*

Approximately three months is probably the earliest time as a team that you can do an adequate look-back to review where you and the team were when you started, and what you have become. Sufficient time has passed within which to have made some progress as a team, and yet it is also a short enough time that you can correct any issues or derailments.

● *Being able to celebrate the experiences you had:*

You and your team set out to achieve key outcomes by the end of 100 days, and you will have had many experiences of success and learning along the way. By bringing your process to a close at the end of 100 days, it gives you guys an excuse to mark the occasion with a celebration. The celebration itself will signal to the team that hard work is recognised, and it is also an opportunity for further team bonding and fun.

Reset your team's desired outcomes for the longer term. The First 100 Days Team Plan has served its purpose. You and your team strived to achieve desired outcomes relevant to the end of 100 days. Now you and your team need to reset new desired outcomes for the longer term.

Open yourself and the team up to the new possibilities. Now that the team has achieved growth in the past 100 days, what are the new possibilities? Perhaps your ideas were limited at the beginning, and now you have learned new things about each other and the role, and new possibilities need to be discussed.

The First 100 Days Team Plan got you here, so where are you and your team going next?

2 Record team achievements and capture lessons learned

When you started out with this team, you had an end in mind and key interim milestones to be achieved by you and your team along the way. Now is the time to record what was achieved in terms of those desired outcomes. Were team stakeholder expectations met, and what did you and your team learn along the way?

The task of writing a 'record of achievement' requires time out to consider whether your team has:

● delivered early results;
● achieved growth and developed skills;
● met or exceeded stakeholder expectations.

This process of recording achievements and lessons learned will:

● assist in forward-planning;
● give team members a confidence boost and a sense of pride in their accomplishments;
● motivate the team to do even better moving forward.

The act of writing the record of achievement shows that you place a value on the process of your learning and growth as a team. Assign somebody on your team to meet with each team member, elicit the information, write the record of achievement and share it at the next team meeting. Then it is not a case of you 'telling' the team what was achieved, but a more bottom-up collaborative process whereby the team agree what was achieved and where the opportunities are for team learning, growth and next steps.

discover what people are proud of

Team members should be empowered to record any achievement that they feel proud of. Discovering what people are proud of offers you the opportunity to learn more about what matters to team members. These form important clues for you on how to motivate team members to achieve even higher performance.

RECORD OF TEAM ACHIEVEMENTS
@END OF THE FIRST 100 DAYS

At macro level

Evidence of what the team has delivered against its role and purpose

Evidence that the team has met or exceeded stakeholder expectations

Key team achievements over the past 100 days

Key lessons learned

At micro level

Achievements versus each of the First 100 Days Team Plan desired outcomes

---

▶

Per team member

What are you most proud of in
terms of the team's achievements
in the past 100 days?

3 Communicate team success to stakeholders

Essentially this team exists to serve its stakeholders. The end of
the first 100 days is a timely opportunity to PR yourselves as a
team and to remind your stakeholders what you have achieved
over the whole past three months.

**what value was
delivered to
stakeholders by
this team in the
past 100 days?**

Orientate your team to think about
the past 100 days purely from a
stakeholder perspective and ask
yourself: what value was delivered to
stakeholders by this team in the past
100 days?

WHY COMMUNICATE TEAM SUCCESS?

Pro-active communication reassures stakeholders that you and
your team are in control, striving to achieve high standards
and keen to deliver on your commitments. In cases where any
disgruntled or difficult stakeholder is questioning the value
of the team, then this is your opportunity to pro-actively
communicate and evidence your value-add, without appearing
to be defensive.

Sharing team success with stakeholders:

- keeps stakeholders informed, supportive, enthusiastic;
- impresses stakeholders with a list of early team wins;
- reminds stakeholders of your value-add as a team;
- builds confidence of stakeholders in the team;
- provides an opportunity to address needs, interests, concerns;
- secures new projects/assignments, and/or secures more budget and resources;
- manages stakeholder expectations going forward.

HOW TO COMMUNICATE TEAM SUCCESS

Know your audience. Your messages will be most effective when you are aware of your recipients' different styles. Do they prefer:

- detail or high-level summary?
- flashy presentation or one-pager document?
- email, social media or face to face?

The most impactful form of stakeholder communication and engagement is face to face. Email is usually the least valuable. And remember that the tone we use when we communicate can be even more important than what we communicate – so be energetic in your tone, and communicate success and optimism about the team in terms of both what you say, and how you say it.

4 Celebrate with your team

A team celebration will improve the 'feel good' factor of being a member of this team. Celebrations enhance a sense of belonging, and contribute towards building good team spirit.

Team celebrations serve a number of constructive purposes:

- as a marker between the end of one journey and the beginning of another;
- as an opportunity to acknowledge individual team member contributions;
- as an affirmation of early wins and early successes as a team;
- as a motivator to achieve more wins and more successes as a team;
- as a reason for a social event and team-bonding event;
- simply to say 'thank you' to the team for their support and a job well done.

motivated individuals are those that feel they are making progress towards their goals

Motivated individuals are those that feel they are making progress towards their goals, so marking the team's progress at the end of the first 100 days should be an important part of your team's motivation strategy.

This next suggestion might sound like an odd thing to say, but I suggest you tell your team that this is a celebration of the team successes and the team failures. It would be great, if as leader of the team, you can reframe 'failures' as learning experiences – and that you genuinely mean this. After all, if you guys don't fail then perhaps you're not taking enough risks or stretching yourselves hard enough. If you and your team members didn't make mistakes from time to time, then individually and collectively you would not be learning.

Being mature enough to acknowledge the opportunity that failures present in terms of learning opportunities sends a very positive message of trust to your team. Your team should not be afraid of you, afraid of failing or afraid of making mistakes. Everybody – including you – fails from time to time, and makes mistakes from time to time. Your people will become more loyal and develop greater trust in you if they know that you are understanding of occasional mistakes, misunderstandings, errors of judgement and if they feel secure that you will give them another chance.

The work persona of individual team members may mean that some people present themselves as very formal and serious individuals in the workplace, whereas when there is a celebration event, you might find that the formal barriers break down and people relax and open up a little. When people are in a more relaxed setting, the communication amongst team members will improve. At away days, or at social occasions, people meet each other from a different perspective. Team members discover shared interests that they never realised existed. If it is a fun event, people will refer back to the memory afterwards. The atmosphere on the team can be more open and trusting, and job performance will improve.

Knowing how to have fun as a team is important. Enjoy!

5 Reset team objectives and renew the endeavour

The first 100 days offered you a time-bound opportunity to see what the team could do. It was a sprint to achieve desired outcomes within a fixed period, and your team endeavoured to achieve its goals with this deadline in mind. The new beginning was the burning platform for the First 100 Days Team Plan, so now what is the new platform for change and renewed team endeavour?

Rather than lurch from 100 days to 100 days, which is too short-termist, think about a relevant longer length of time such as end of the new financial year, or end of the calendar year, or any other relevant end point according to your strategic context, for the next key team deadline for achievements.

RESET TEAM OBJECTIVES

Apply the underlying principles that I used to assist you on creating the First 100 Days Team Plan, to create your new medium- or longer-term team plan. Essentially, you need to:

- be clear on the leadership goal and timeline;
- write your new team plan;
- set up your accountability mechanism;
- build your support system.

Be clear on the leadership goal and timeline
Reset the medium-term goal and the timeline for renewed endeavour.

For example: 'The team has achieved 10 new desired outcomes by the end of the calendar year.'

Write your new team plan
Establish a new set of priority areas. In the context of your new beginning as leader of the team, I offered you a set of priority areas in terms of the seven-part success formula. For the new strategic platform and context, you and your team will have to agree on the new set of priority areas. By now, your team has gelled, and is higher performing and higher functioning and can take more ownership in terms of setting its own priority areas.

Start with the end in mind: what is your desired outcome to be achieved by the end of the new time period on each priority area?

Set up your accountability mechanism

Establish key milestone review points. Perhaps these become every quarter end, instead of every month end. Assign co-owners with responsibility to achieve each desired outcome.

Build your support system

Enlist expert advice/support for the journey. Find useful mentors or consultants who can give you advice and that extra edge on team performance.

RENEW THE ENDEAVOUR

The First 100 Days Team Plan is a device for how to get off to a very productive and accelerated start with your team. It is useful by itself, because it focuses everyone on a clear direction, it brings the team's stakeholders on the journey and it is all about getting fast results. Getting off to a fast and productive start allows you and the team to create a very positive momentum for the rest of your time together.

There is also a very important leadership learning subtext taking place. The whole First 100 Days Team Plan experience has been about honing your leadership skills and helping you to become a better leader beyond the first 100 days.

The very act of developing and implementing your First 100 Days Team Plan will have improved your leadership skills on:

- being more strategic;
- structured planning;
- teaming/collaboration;
- stakeholder management;
- emotional intelligence with groups;
- delivering fast results.

you should now feel better equipped and more empowered to tackle any future leadership challenges

These are new or newly honed leadership skills that you can take with you onto the next phase of your journey with your team, and onto your next leadership promotion. You should now feel better equipped and more empowered to tackle any future leadership challenges.

Congratulations on completing your First 100 Days with your team.

Final words

Leading a team in your first 100 days is not easy. You have a lot to deal with as a newly appointed leader – getting up to speed with your role requirements, building a good relationship with your boss, meeting new stakeholders, possibly navigating a new organisation or geographic culture.

It is understandable, with so much to deal with, that it can be challenging to invest adequate time and effort needed to build a high performing team. Plus team members are exhausting, you can never give your people enough time and energy – they always want more! This is why I wrote the book. I wanted you to know that I get it. It is not easy. But if you plan in advance, try to assimilate the insights, and recognise that 'leading your team in the first 100 days' is a skill, then you can at least start to hone that skill. With every new role experience you will get better and better at it. No one is the perfect leader, but if you are at least striving for high standards then you are better than most.

let's face it: the quality of leadership in the world is not great

Let's face it: the quality of leadership in the world is not great. As a human race, we need the people in charge – our leaders – to strive to do better. We could all be doing a much better job within our own domain of responsibility on this Earth. If individually, we all tried to do a better job within our own humble areas of responsibility, then maybe as a human race we could collectively raise our game.

This is your moment. This is your opportunity to raise your own game as a leader and role model your efforts to your team and other people inside and outside your organisation. If you demonstrate great leadership – or even attempts at great leadership – then your teams will learn from you and all your efforts and will be copied and replicated. You have more power than you realise. Everyone always remembers that great person who once led them. Be that person that team members talk about for years to come. Be that person that people admire and try to emulate.

Every new role beginning is an opportunity to renew and start again on the path to being the best leader you can be. Seize the opportunity, lead your team well in the first 100 days, and success will follow.

Thank you for reading this book and good luck on your journey.

Index

accelerate on arrival 55–75
  advice from top executives 72–5
  avoiding the leader-as-hero trap
    63–6
  bringing in `SWAT team'
    re-enforcements 66–8
  launching the Team Plan 56–63
  leader-team bonding 68–72
accountability
  lack of 106
  mechanisms 155
action-oriented communication 111
Alvarez, Luis 73
Anson, Lisa 142
assertive leadership 140–1
authentic leadership 58
autonomy
  giving to team members 41

barriers to high performance 101–8
  fear of conflict 105–6
  group think 107–8
  inadequate systems and
    technology 104–5
  lack of commitment 106
  lack of trust 105
  no accountability 107
  silo-thinking 106
  unclear roles and responsibilities
    104
  weak leadership 101–2
  wrong mission 102
  wrong people 102–3
behavioural intelligence 130
Bion's Theory of Groups 82, 84
Bishop, Phil 116

Breslin, Paul 117
Buekers, John 95

celebrations of success 151–3
CEO agenda
  and company strategy 22, 23
change agents 90–1, 92
clique behaviour 105
closing out the Team Plan 146–8
Coburn, John 116
communicator
  @60 days 108–11
  action-oriented 111
  clarity of communication 108–9
  communicating team success to
    150–1
  communication style 59–60
  detailed communication 39
  and emotional awareness 111
  and empathy 110
  and engagement 110
  and the final 10 days 125, 126
  stakeholder concerns 38–9
  team concerns 38
  and team members 92–3
  and the Team Plan 30, 38–40, 50,
    53
  launching 59–60
  timing of communication
    109–10
  transparency 110–11
  two-way communication 39–40,
    110
company vision & strategy 22–4
  and team mission 25
competitor team behaviour 13–14

conflict
    dealing with 123
    fear of 105–6
    feedback about conflict issues 137
    in groups 86
consensus-building 141
consultants 67–8, 155

debriefing with your hiring manager
    12–13
delegation 94
dependency
    and group dysfunction 84
Dhinsa, Jojar 142
direct reports xix, 10, 11
    presentations from 14–16
    recruiting 36
Djaba, Magnus 74
Dobson-Smith, Dan 74
dotted line reports xix, 10
dysfunctional group behaviours see
    group dysfunction

early research 6, 10–14
emotional awareness 111
emotional focus 6, 7–10, 13
emotional intelligence 7, 130, 155
empathy 110
executive advice
    @30 days 94–6
    @60 days 115–17
    @90 days 142–3
    on arrival 72–5
executive search consultants 67–8
executors 90, 91, 92
external consultants 66–8, 123
    and team to leader feedback 133–5

face-to-face communication
    of team success 151
facilitators
    and team to leader feedback 133–5

failures, celebration of 152
fast results xvi–xvii
feedback 127–36
    leader to team 127–9
    individual team members
        129–32
    stakeholder to team 132–3
    team reflection on 136–41
    team to leader 133–6
feedback-sandwiches 128–9
fight or flight
    and group dysfunction 85
finance analysts/consultants 68
finishing your First 100 days 145–56
    celebrating with your team 151–3
    closing out the Team Plan 146–8
    communicating team success to
        stakeholders 150–1
    recording team achievements
        148–50
    resetting team objectives 153–5
    reviewing the endeavour 155
First100 consultants 67
First 100 Days, meaning of xxv–xxvi
Fuller, Bob 74–5

game plans 16
Gartside, Richard 116
George, Pter 74
goals
    resetting team objectives 153–5
    setting 42
    strategic 24
Goldberg, Judy 96
Golding, Andrew 115
goodwill from team members 15
Griffiths-Lambert, Kate 95
group dysfunction 82–9
    and Basic Assumptions 84–7
    dependency 84
    fight or flight 85
    me-ness 86–7

one-ness 86
subversion 87–9
teams going off task 83–4
group think 107–8, 124

Handley, John 116
hard skills 44
Harker, John 115
Harrison, Jean 96
hero behaviours 63–6, 104
Hindley, David 143
hiring managers
debriefing with 12–13
home workers xix, 11
Hood, Ian 117
hot desking xix
HR (human resources)
removing underperformers 104
and subversion 88
and team recruitment 36–7

individual feedback 129–32
intellectual intelligence 130
intelligence ranking
and individual feedback to team
members 130–1
internet
emailing a prearrival memo 16–18
Googling yourself 16
IT systems, inadequate 104–5

Johnson, Faran 142

knowledge intelligence 130

launching the Team Plan 56–63
communicator 59–60
mission setter 58–9
motivator 60
preparing for the workshop 56–7
recruiter 59
review mechanism 62–3

role model 57–8
sense-checking 62
skills builder 60–1
target maker 61–2
Laurence, Guy 72–3
leader to team feedback 127–9
leader-as-hero 63–6, 104
leader-team bonding 44, 68–72, 99,
123
and effective leadership 140–1
leader–team relationships
increasing complexity of xviii–xix
LeaderTeam Success formula 30–46,
52–3
communicator 30, 38–40, 49, 53
mission setter 30, 32–5, 49
motivator 30, 40–2, 49
recruitment 30, 35–8
role model 30, 31–2, 49
skills builder 30, 42–3, 49
target maker 30, 44–6, 49
leadership 101–2
assertive 140–1
authentic 58
change fatigue xix–xx
controlling 113–15
emotional focus on style of 8–9
feedback on 134–6
handover 20–2
honing your leadership skills
155–6, 157
raising your game as a leader 157–8
reflecting on 140–1
role models 30, 31–2, 49, 53,
57–8
roles and responsibilities xv
expansion of xviii
unclear 104
tenures xvi–xviii
weak 101–2
leveraging your team xx–xxi
listening and communicating 39–40

McElvaney, Paul 74
Maclean, Elaine 115
Martin, Clare 95
maternity leavers 11
me-ness
    and group dysfunction 86–7
meetings
    checking if the team is on task 82–3
    virtual team meetings xix
    see also workshops
memos, pre-arrival 16–18
Millership, Marcus 142
mission setter
    and the final 10 days 125, 126
    preparations 24–6
    team mission
        examples of statements 34–5
        wrong 102
    and the Team Plan 30, 32–5, 53
        launching 58–9
    and team rebuilding 33
motivator xx, 30, 40–2
    and the final 10 days 125
    and skills-building 44
    and the Team Plan 30, 40–2
        launching 60
Murdoch, Shiree 142

new technologies 92
90Day milestone 121–43
    executive advice 142–3
    feedback and issues to be aired
        127–36
    team reflection on 136–41
    the final 10 days, writing the
        'to-do' list 124–6
    and the Team Plan 48, 50, 52–3
    reviewing progress against
        122–4
Noren, Pontus 95

O'Flynn, Denis 95

one-ness 86

pairing
    and group dysfunction 85
part-time workers xix, 11
PAs (personal assistants)
    and subversion 88
performance
    annual cycle of appraisal 11–12
    see also barriers to high
        performance
Philipps, Ian 75
predecessors 12
    arranging a swift leadership
        handover 20–2
    staying on as a team member
        21–2
preparations 5–28
    early research 6, 10–14
    emotional focus 6, 7–10, 13
        relax and rejuvenate 9–10
    leadership handover 20–2
    meeting the team informally 19
    team mission 24–6
    for the Team Plan Workshop 56–7
    team presentations 14–16
    understanding the strategic
        context 22–4
    writing a pre-arrival memo 16–18
presentations
    from direct reports 14–16
previous co-workers
    recruiting 37

recording team achievements 148–50
recruiter
    bringing in fresh talent 11
    and feedback to team members
        131
    and the final 10 days 125, 126
    replacing the whole team 43
    and the Team Plan 30, 35–8, 50, 53

launching 59
redundancies, timing of
    communicating 110
relax and rejuvenate 9–10
reputation
    and team performance xx–xxi
research
    early 6, 10–14
resetting team objectives 153–5
results intelligence 130
rewards
    and motivation 41, 42
role model
    and the final 10 days 125–6
    and the Team Plan 30, 31–2, 49, 53
    launching 57–8
Ryding, James 94

self-awareness 7
    and team recruitment 35–6
self-regulation 7
silo-thinking 106
60-Day milestone 97–117
    communication 108–11
    executive advice 115–17
    removing barriers to high
        performance 101–8
    and the Team Plan 48, 50, 53–4
        reviewing progress against
        98–100
        updating 112–13
skills builder
    and the final 10 days 125, 126
    and the Team Plan 30, 42–3, 53
    launching 60–1
soft skills 44
speed as a competitive business
    weapon xvi–xvii
stakeholders xix, xx
    and the 60 days Team Workshop
        100
    closing out the Team Plan 146

communication with 38–9
    and team success 150–1
    feedback from 132–3
    and mission setting 33
    and records of achievement 148
    and target making 45, 126
    and team reputation and
        performance xx
standard-setting 31–2
strategic context and timeline 22–4
strategic intelligence 130
strategic thinkers 90, 91, 92
strategy consultants 68
stress
    and emotional focus 7
subversion
    and group dysfunction 87–9
support systems 155
Swantee, Olaf 73
`SWAT team' reenforcement's 66–8

talent spotters 37
target maker
    and the final 10 days 125, 126
    and the Team Plan 30, 44–6, 50, 53
    launching 61–2
targets
    team mission and team targets
        25–6
team matrix 131–2
team mediators 123
team members
    accountability of 106
    building consensus with 141
    capitalising on the strengths of
        89–93
    celebrating with 151–3
    change agents 90–1, 92
    commitment of 106
    communication with 108–10
    on job security 40, 59
    early research on 10–14

team members (continued)
empathy with 7–8
executors 90, 91, 92
existing passions of 92
fear of conflict 105–6
game plans 16
group think 107–8, 124
helping to shine 26–8
individual feedback to 129–32
lack of trust in 105
leader-team bonding 68–72, 99,
123
and effective leadership 140–1
and leadership change fatigue
xix–xx
organisation structure chart 10
preparing for your arrival 14–19
reflection on feedback 136–41
replacing the whole team 43
reputation and performance
xx–xxi
resetting team objectives 153–5
silothinking 106–7
strategic thinkers 90, 91, 92
and the Team Plan
assigning co-owners 50–1
motivating factors 41–2
skills building 30, 42–3
target making 45–6
unclear roles and responsibilities
104
underperformers 40, 93, 103–4
weekly updates from 63
wrong people 102–3
team mission 24–6
wrong 102
Team Plan xxi, xxiii, 29–53
checking if the team is on task 82–3
closing out 146–8
launching 56–63
Leader-Team Success formula
30–46, 52–3

new team plan (after the First 100
Days) 154
reviewing progress against
@30 days 80–2
@60 days 98–100
@90 days 122–4
checking on strengths of team
members 92–3
updating
@30 Days 93–4
@60 Days 112
writing the plan 46–53
assigning co-owners 50–1
breaking down the desired
outcome 47–9
first step actions 48, 49, 52–3
sense-checking and
completing 51
starting with the end in mind 47
sub-outcomes 48, 49, 52–3
team targets 25–6
teaming intelligence 130
technical intelligence 130
tenures of leadership roles xvi–xviii
30-Day milestone 79–96
capitalising on the strengths of
the team 89–93
executive advice 94–6
spotting dysfunctional group
behaviours 82–9
sense-checking 82–3
and the Team Plan 48, 50, 53–4
reviewing progress against
80–2
training 42
skills building 44
underperformers 103
transparency in communication
110–11
trust, lack of 105

underperformers 40, 93, 103–4

virtual team members xix, 10

Waight, Mark 116
Walker, Nikki 143
walking the floor 70
Warren, Guy 73
Williams, Lisa 74
Williams, Tony 142
Wilson, Keith 115
Woollard, Stuart 95
workshops
    @30 Days Team 81–2, 93–4

@60 Days Team 98–100
@90 Days Team 122–4, 127
launching the Team Plan 56–63
see also meetings
Wright, Andrew 73
wrong people 102–3
wrong team mission 102

Your First 100 Days: how to make
    maximum impact in
    your new leadership role
    xxvi–xxviii

Notes

Also by
Niamh O'Keeffe

"An insightful 100 minutes read for a great First 100 Days."
Sander van't Noordende, Group Chief Executive of Management
Consulting, Accenture.

"A structured and disciplined approach to transitioning into
a new role that recognises both the practical and emotional
challenges. Will help you get off to a fast and focused start."
Alan McIntyre, Chief Operating Officer, Oliver Wyman Group.

"Provides a practical and challenging framework to give senior
executives the support they need in their first 100 days."
Tony Hanway, Director, Telefonica O2

Read on

9780273732044

9780273729860

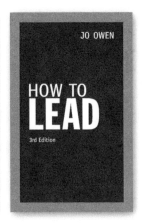

9780273759614

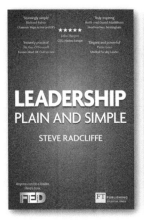

9780273772415

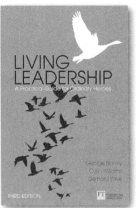

9780273772163

9780273776802

Available now online and at all good bookstores
www.pearson-books.com